The Young Child's Memory for Words

* * *

DEVELOPING
FIRST AND SECOND LANGUAGE
AND LITERACY

Daniel R. Meier

TEACHERS COLLEGE PRESS

Teachers College, Columbia University
New York and London

Published by Teachers College Press, 1234 Amsterdam Avenue, New York, NY 10027

Library of Congress Cataloging-in-Publication Data

Meier, Daniel R.
    The young child's memory for words : developing first and second language and literacy / Daniel R. Meier.
        p. cm.
    Includes bibliographical references and index.
    ISBN 0-8077-4430-1 (cloth : alk. paper) — ISBN 0-8077-4429-8 (pbk. : alk. paper)
    1. Language acquisition.   2. Literacy.   3. Memory.   I. Title.
P118.7.M45   2004
401'.93—dc22   2003065012

ISBN 0-8077-4429-8 (paper)
ISBN 0-8077-4430-1 (cloth)

Printed on acid-free paper
Manufactured in the United States of America

11   10   09   08   07   06   05   04   8   7   6   5   4   3   2   1

The Young Child's Memory for Words

*   *   *

DEVELOPING
FIRST AND SECOND LANGUAGE
AND LITERACY

for my daughter, Kaili

Contents

Acknowledgments

I thank all the children, families, and teachers with whom I have worked. They greatly helped make this book possible, and I appreciate their willingness to work with me as we try to strengthen our literacy education for young children. As always, the children have been wonderful—drawing and writing in their journals, discussing books, working with one another, and asking me to read their favorite books.

I also wish to thank the anonymous reviewers who reviewed the initial proposal for this book. I also thank Susan Britsch and Deborah Luna for reading early drafts of the book. Eve Gregory, Connie Jubb, and Rosario Villasana-Ruiz also took the time to read the book and provided comments —thank you. Thanks also to Carol Copple at NAEYC for her helpful editing and revisions. The preschool of the University of Hawai'i at Manoa kindly provided permission to use a photograph of their classroom. Thanks also go to the following teachers for granting me permission to use examples from their teaching: Vivian Alipio, Jessica Bantegui, Jan Duckart, Evangeline Espiritu, Jessica Fickle, Kathy Forhan, Hazelle Fortich, Marianne Geronimo, Muriel Johnson, Rivka Mason, Hazel Mesina, Tom Prince, Manuel Kichi Wong, Cathy Richardson, Mozhgan Sayfadini, Kayoko Seto, Kristin Thurmond, Joseph P. Villaluz, Norma Villazana-Price, Mary Weese, and Alonzo Williams. Thanks, also, to Monteverde School.

Brian Ellerbeck and Susan Liddicoat of Teachers College Press supported and guided me from beginning to end with this book. Brian has remained wonderfully supportive of my writing, and Susan provided me with careful and sensitive editing suggestions for strengthening the book's content and form. Thanks, too, to Karl Nyberg for carefully guiding the book through the production stage.

My parents and my brothers—thank you for your continued support and encouragement.

And Hazelle, my wife, thank you for giving me the time and energy to finish the book. This book took a little longer to write than I thought it would, partly because our daughter, Kaili, turned 2, then 3, and then 4 years old, and we had more waking hours to spend time together. And this really is a reminder of what I am trying to do with this book—to talk about literacy as a dynamic human relationship that takes time, dedication, and care.

Toward a Memory for Literacy

MR. MEIER: Are you reading the words [in the book] or memorizing it?
CIERRA (PRESCHOOLER): I'm reading the words *and* memorizing it!

When Kaili, my daughter, was about 8 months old, my friend Paul came over to our house to visit. Paul also had a young child, loved children, and playfully interacted with my daughter. At one point, Paul tried to get Kaili to dance a little with him on the living-room rug. For an infant who could not walk, let alone dance, I thought this a bit too much of a new endeavor for her. I thought to myself, "Oh my, what is he doing? She's only 8 months old." But I noticed that Kaili enjoyed Paul's encouragement and attempts to get her to dance.

"That's OK," said Paul, "it's beyond her for the moment, but now she has a *memory* for dancing. Now she has an idea of what dancing is."

Later on I thought about how Paul's comment on memory applied to young children's literacy development. I had been thinking about the current emphasis, in preschool and the primary grades both in the United States and abroad, on literacy standards and assessment. Paul's comment helped me, as a teacher, to step back and to think about the big picture of who children are, how they develop and learn, and the most sensible ways to foster children's language and literacy growth.

LITERACY AS A JOURNEY OF MEMORY

In our contemporary preschool and primary-grade classrooms, the challenges of teaching and learning remain complicated and occasionally mysterious—and always requiring lots of hard work and thinking on the part of educators, children, and their families. It is not only children who all learn in their own individual ways, according to their own pace and inclination; so do we as adult teachers and learners. We, too, have our own developmental trajectories that influence how much we can (and want) to take on in our literacy teaching, and how much we can incorporate current expectations regarding literacy standards and assessment.

Memory, both as a real part of our own literacy learning and as a metaphor for seeing new ways to teach, plays both a subtle and an obvious role in this process. Young children's memories for language and literacy are newer and more fresh than ours. This freshness of memory can bring on the potential joys of language and literacy as children discover and de-light in their first words, their first stories, their first books. They immedi-ately take to a funny new storybook character and want to read the same book over and over again—they want to solidify the newness of the literacy experience and make it a memory for themselves. These kinds of memo-ries for literacy are based on positive and successful experiences with lit-eracy. In other situations, though, memories for literacy are less positive and less likely to stick with children. In these instances, children are asked to understand and use literacy in ways that are too challenging for them, or are simply boring and do not entice children to use their imaginations or creativity, or even spark their interest.

If we want to change and strengthen our literacy education, we as teachers can start by considering our own literacy memories. As adults, we have the power to make more sense of and gain more control over our lan-guage and literacy memories. Our memories have been with us for a longer period of time, and we have the luxury of picking and choosing which memories to keep and which to change, add, or discard. Our memories are a never-ending compilation of our personal and professional lives, a layer-ing of all the words from our school days, the languages of our homes and communities, the experiences of our professional teaching lives. For some of us, the boundaries and borders of our literacy memories are hard to see and hear again, and we can only recall and revisit them through some sud-den jarring of the mind and heart. We might, for instance, suddenly remem-ber a song our grandmother sang to us when we were infants as we stumble upon a book containing the song. This is a long-ago memory coming round quickly and suddenly to us, as if we turned the corner and walked right into it.

Sometimes of course we are glad for this sudden rush of memories—they reunite us with our former (and younger) selves and take us back to places and situations to which we would like to go again. We were not expecting it, and in this sense, our literacy memories retain some of the fresh-ness and vividness of children's brand-new memories for words and books. This is the important developmental connection that we have with children; we can revisit our old memories, almost pretending that they are new ones, and in the process we can reexperience what literacy learning might be like for preschoolers and kindergartners.

Traditional memory terminology and concepts such as *short-term* and *long-term* memory are important for fostering successful literacy learning. My use of *memory* in literacy education, though, is different. First, I am inter-ested in a child-driven meaning for the role of memory in literacy teaching and learning, something more intimately tied to children's developmental capabilities, their ways of talking and experiencing books, their particular personalities and socially and culturally influenced literacy interests. In this view of memory, teaching is less incremental and linear and more circular and dynamic—we move forward, backward, and sideways as we learn to sense, experience, and adjust our teaching to our children. Second, memory for literacy is tied to literary aspects of talking, reading, writing—character, plot, words, symbols, color, light, sound, silence, movement, voice, and action. Third, memory pertains to literacy knowledge (such as identifying the letter names of the alphabet) and literacy skill (orchestrating or putting literacy knowledge together into practice). Both the immediate and ultimate goal of literacy education is not the learning of skills, but rather, sophisticated and complex experiences in experimenting, manipulating, and using varied oral and written language forms. Learning to identify the sounds and letters of the alphabet, for instance, is not an end in itself. It is actually rather low-level literacy knowledge that will remain low level unless powerfully linked with the higher level skill of telling a story, discussing the plot of a book, or dramatizing a story.

Fourth, creating memories for literacy needs to be seen as a complicated process. It cannot be tied to the age or grade levels of children, or a step-by-step incremental view of how children learn literacy. In other words, if we believe that young children of preschool age need low-level or "basic" literacy knowledge for the literacy rigors of kindergarten, then we are not making the most of the preschool years. Whether children are 3 years old or 6 years old, they need enriching and engaging literacy activities that speak to who they are at the moment. Literacy education cannot be dictated by what children need to learn at some point ahead of where they are—if this is the case, we'll always be playing catch-up.

Fifth, memory for literacy is immediately and ultimately tied to the here and now of children's lives and worlds. For instance, we often find ourselves focused on teaching something at a certain time to certain children (for instance, explaining the meaning of a "phosphorescent sea" from William Steig's *Amos and Boris*), but what are we really doing? While we pay attention to where we want children to be and go in their literacy learning, they are often not with us. They want to be friends with one another and with the characters in a book. So in reading *Amos and Boris*, we are not so much just "doing literacy" as intermingling the book with children's lives—reading, talking, and sharing a particular story and world of language that helps us see friendship in new and valuable ways. To allow memories for literacy to take hold, we must open children's eyes and ears to the newness, the attraction, and the delight of a new story of friendship and of beholding a "phosphorescent sea."

MEMORY AND LITERACY STANDARDS

We know that good teaching touches the immediacy of children's learning and engagement. We know that this is our point of contact and where real learning happens. Unfortunately, what is problematic about the current emphasis on literacy standards and expectations is that we are asked to do more in a shorter period of time; to squash the experience of literacy into smaller developmental compartments. This leaves less time and room for creating memories that might stretch beyond the preschool or kindergarten year. But children's development—and we can see this from what and how they learn *outside* of school (for instance, in learning to dress themselves, tie their shoes, use the bathroom, use a knife and fork, ride a bike)—so often defies time constraints. Often without our knowing it, children create their own literacy memories, which prove hard to see and hold on to, and may not actually surface for a long period of time. We can design and create environments, materials, methods, and strategies to bring about instantaneous acquisition of literacy knowledge and the skillful display of this knowledge—and this would be in accordance with current literacy standards—but it is an effort that ultimately narrows the possibilities for high-quality literacy instruction. Powerful literacy teaching is teaching for memory, memories for now and memories to carry with us.

Much of current literacy policy advocates preparing preschool children with a literacy foundation ("preliteracy skills") for learning to read and write in kindergarten and beyond. In this view, the *pre* has been taken out of *preschool* and joined with the more formal reading and writing instruction of kindergarten and the primary grades. This perspective is based on the idea that if children are not well prepared in preschool, and remember what they have been taught, then they will be ill prepared to learn to read and write in the primary grades. But, unfortunately, there is no preliteracy, just as there is no prewalking or prebicycling or prethinking. For sure, we listen to words and crawl and use training wheels—these are developmental steps toward greater orchestration of our knowledge in these areas—but to children (and the accompanying adults) it is *already* sophisticated and challenging. There really is nothing *pre-* about it. If seen this way, preschool literacy education can be reconceptualized to serve the language and literacy needs of preschoolers as they are and to base primary-grade literacy education on the needs and talents of the particular kindergartners rather than where they need to be in Grade 1 and beyond.

A view of literacy as "preliteracy" (preschool) and as learning to read and write (kindergarten and first grade) is really a watered-down version of the possibilities of literacy for children. If we as adult learners want to improve our own language and literacy learning, we may choose a basic composition class or a class on Latin American writers, or we may take both, giving us a class on fundamental writing knowledge and one on the creativity and imagination of wonderful writers and storytellers. The same breadth and depth of skill, knowledge, engagement, and wonderment that we seek as adults should be provided for young children. We must constantly fight the understandable urge to simplify literacy education and therefore make it mechanical, rote, and geared toward low-level and short-term memory.

The current emphasis on literacy standards is helpful to a certain extent. Standards can give us something to aspire to and base our teaching on. They provide clear, concrete teaching goals for breaking down those basic elements of literacy (such as identifying letter sounds) that many children need as they become readers and writers. But we also need to control the standards, move and shake them into language and literacy teaching that makes good developmental and teaching sense for us, our children, and our families. We need literacy education that goes beyond a mechanical view of reading and writing, and toward literacy teaching as a creative endeavor. We want children to become lifelong readers and writers.

The new literacy standards are especially problematic for English-language learners (children learning English as a new language), who need particular forms of literacy support. Given the dramatic decrease in bilingual opportunities for these children to speak, read, and write in their first language, English-language learners are asked to read and write in a new language, at a faster rate, and earlier than ever before. We are faced with the formidable task not only of teaching to the new literacy standards, but also of helping English-language learners to speak, read, and write within the sights and sounds of another language. Further, a number of these children are from immigrant families who are often unfamiliar with general schooling and educational practices and expectations in the United States. So we have the multilevel challenge of helping English-language learners to learn English (if bilingual opportunities are not available) and learn the social and academic parameters of American classroom life. We need much more than standards to do this well.

For English-language learners without access to bilingual or multilingual education in schools, we must create lasting literacy memories in a new and unfamiliar language. One day I worked with Diana, a Spanish-speaking kindergartner in an English-medium classroom, on identifying a group of 10 letters and sounds in English. Diana kept getting stuck on the same four or five letters, and when we continued to practice identifying them, she would identify them correctly but then not recognize them a few minutes later. This was frustrating for both of us. Her difficulty could be seen as a problem with short-term memory or auditory and visual discrimination or Spanish-English language interference. Most likely, though, it was a collection of factors that included learning the sounds of a new language, learning to isolate sounds and letters (not as common a practice in Spanish literacy), and the overall developmental task of focusing on letters for a 5-year-old. What was I trying to do as the teacher? Teach the isolated sounds and letter names—that this letter shape was called a *b* and that it made these sounds in English (though it sounded similar to the *v* in the Spanish word *vamos*) and that this letter shape called *a* made these different sounds. This was the beginning of a yearlong process of engaging Diana with the sounds and sights of a new language.

LITERACY EDUCATION—WHERE DO WE WANT IT TO GO?

Standards and assessment alone don't make for excellent teaching. Teachers do. We need to improve literacy education through structural changes (smaller class sizes, smaller schools, more funding) and better materials and resources (books, curriculum programs, technology), but these gains will not be long lasting without a steady strengthening of the human element in teaching. We need a vision for literacy that enables us to think for ourselves and with our children and families. We can adapt general literacy standards to fit our local teaching and community contexts. If we are told that we must use a particular published reading series or literacy program at our site or school, we need the political will and the educational vision to translate these materials and goals for the particular children that we teach. We can find wiggle room within the standards to tinker at the edges, giving a prominent daily place to story time and read-alouds, sharing time and show-and-tell, dictation, talking in a variety of Englishes, group writing, multicultural and multilingual picture books and chapter books, poems, rhymes, fiction and nonfiction, words and stories in many languages, legends, tall tales, reports, drama and plays, puppetry, song and dance, call and response, talk story, charades and pantomime, and moments of quiet and silence.

There is now more pressure than ever on early childhood and primary-grade teachers to teach reading and writing earlier and better. In this pushing down of reading and writing expectations into the younger years, teachers and families are of various minds regarding how to best juggle children's developmental capabilities with these age- and grade-level literacy expectations. Historically, there has been a strong emphasis in early childhood education for preschool to emphasize exploration and play with literacy in informal ways—leaving formal instruction in reading and writing to the primary grades. The leading early childhood educational and professional organizations, such as the National Association for the Education of Young Children (NAEYC), and other advocates of progressive education have long advocated a play-based curriculum that promotes children's discovery of and experimentation with language and literacy. In recent years, this long-standing tradition has changed somewhat. Books and reading and writing activities have gained a more prominent place in early childhood centers and preschools, and early childhood literature and research sees a more prominent role for literacy in children's successful early childhood learning. Possibly the most dramatic changes have occurred in kindergarten, which in the United States has typically been the transitional year between the play- and socialization-based preschool and the formal reading and writing instruction of first grade. There is now a particularly strong emphasis on helping all children, and especially "at-risk" children with less-than-high-quality or no preschool experiences, not only to get ready to read in kindergarten, but to start reading.

As we reconsider the power of literacy standards to guide teaching, we can shift what we teach and how to more closely match the children whom we teach. Children need language and literacy to fit them, not the other way around. Language and literacy are really connected to the ways that children make friends, solve arguments, think about the phases of the moon, react to a funny story, spell, learn English, hang on to a first language, hold a pencil, and draw lions and faces. Children can and do learn things in isolation, but most children don't. Fostering a memory for words, and lasting and meaningful memories for reading and writing, take into account children's larger encounters with letters, words, sentences, paragraphs, thoughts, ideas, and problems. Diana and I, struggling with *b* and *a*, had to move on to something else (reading a book), and then return later to the letter-identification task. When we returned to our shared challenge, it was easier, and we could resume the joint task of working on the letters and sounds, slowly building up our memories.

It is a simpler policy task to set standards for groups of children than it is to say to teachers and families, "These are your children. We want them to read and write well. But you know them best. Find the ways that work for you and that work for your children; play with the time line of their development as that of learners and yours as that of a teacher, and play with the energy and movement of your old and new memories for reading and writing. You will find your ways as you go along; sometimes you will be together and sometimes you will be apart. That's inevitable." We need, then, more lasting and powerful ways to conceptualize and think about literacy education, and we need small, close-to-home examples of sensitive and sharp teaching and learning connections that help children learn to read and write.

We need children to recognize their *b*s and *a*s, *and* to delight in following a complicated plot from a chapter book, write a poem about their inner wishes, dictate a story about what they want to be when they grow up, develop a sense of voice as an author, and learn information from a nonfiction source. More than a balanced language arts curriculum (for instance, one that balances developing phonemic awareness with appreciating children's literature), we need inspired and energetic teaching that promotes lifelong memories in children for reading and writing.

In preschool and kindergarten literacy, we play critical roles in fostering positive and long-lasting memories for reading, books, words, and written language. High-quality, sophisticated literacy education in preschool is founded on an integration of attention to children's developmental capabilities and their economic, cultural, linguistic, political, and educational realities in and out of school. We cannot deprive children—and this most often applies to children of color and children from low-income backgrounds—of a literacy education that pays attention to the foundational forms and functions of reading and writing. We need to pay careful, sensitive attention to written language that guides young children toward powerful literacy knowledge and a passion and eagerness for long-term connections with books and words.

ABOUT THIS BOOK

This book is about understanding and putting into practice artful ways for children to have long-lasting memories for reading and writing. I offer theoretical and practical ideas for first- and second-language and literacy development of children ages 3 to 6. I hope that both beginning and more experienced teachers will find the book of value as they look at their language arts programs for ways to strengthen their teaching. As a text that combines language and literacy theory and practice, the book is also intended for preschool and elementary administrators and curriculum specialists, researchers in the fields of early childhood education and literacy education, and parents.

Organization of the Book

Each chapter includes an opening set of "Teaching and Learning Questions" and a closing set of "Suggested Activities." The opening questions and the closing activities frame each chapter and create a thread for the book's emphasis on fostering a memory for literacy. The "Activities" are designed for instructors who may be using this book in their college and university classes, and also for individual teachers who are reading this book on their own. I did not put research citations within the text and instead have placed my references at the end of each chapter as "Useful Resources," including children's books cited in the chapter. In the examples of children's talk and literacy, most of the children's names have been changed to provide anonymity, and the use of adult's names follows individual preferences.

In chapter 1, I highlight the building blocks for children's first- and second-language acquisition. The chapter includes a discussion of the language learning of newborns, infants, and toddlers.

In chapter 2, I describe children's first- and second-language learning as a foundation for children's literacy development, and describe programs and practices for promoting children's literacy acquisition during their early school years.

The focus in chapter 3 is on effective strategies for designing and organizing a classroom environment for literacy, and the chapter includes a particular emphasis on selecting and using children's books. At the end of the chapter I include a list of recommended children's books.

In chapter 4, I explain the role of the alphabet in children's literacy learning and describe techniques for integrating alphabet-related activities with children's own interests and resources. A list of recommended alphabet books is included at the end of the chapter.

Chapter 5 is centered on the value of integrating drawing, writing, talking, and dictating for young children's first- and second-language and literacy development.

In chapter 6, I offer a closing discussion on future directions for our early literacy teaching in preschool and the primary grades.

My Perspective and Teaching Background

I currently teach preservice teacher candidates seeking an elementary school teaching credential and experienced teachers pursuing a master's degree in early childhood education at San Francisco State University. My courses focus on language, literacy, narrative and memoir, and teacher research. Much of the children's talk, interaction, and learning that I present and discuss in this book comes from my own teaching experiences working directly with children. The other material comes from preschool and kindergarten colleagues. I have taught elementary and preschool in private and public school settings. I currently serve as a part-time literacy specialist for three kindergarten classrooms at a public K–5 elementary school in the San Francisco East Bay. The kindergarten children with whom I currently work represent a variety of cultural, racial, linguistic, and economic backgrounds. I work with small groups of children considered most in need of extra literacy support. Many of the examples that I use in this book come from my current teaching.

The prevailing literacy policy for preschool and kindergarten favors an emphasis on general standards and expectations. While this has its merits, standards-driven literacy teaching deemphasizes our roles as teachers and discourages the matching of our literacy teaching to our children's particular needs, resources, and interests. If we want to create and foster long-lasting memories for literacy—and encourage children to become lifelong readers and writers and thinkers—we need to go beyond current literacy standards. We need to envision and implement, as best we can in light of the standards, literacy education that is creative, artistic, and inclusive of our talents and those of our children and their families. In this book I present and discuss ideas and strategies for meeting this challenge.

USEFUL RESOURCES

Early Literacy Standards and Expectations

Bredekamp, S., Copple, C., & Neuman, S. B. (2000). *Learning to read and write: Developmentally appropriate practices for young children.* Washington, DC: National Association for the Education of Young Children.

California Child Development Division for Desired Results for Preschool. http://www.cde.ca.gov/cyfsbranch/child_development/

California Department of Education for Kindergarten. http://www.cde.ca.gov/standards/

Robinson, V., Ross, G., & Neal, H. (2000). *Emergent literacy in kindergarten: A review of the research and related suggested activities and learning strategies.* San Mateo, CA: California Kindergarten Association.

Roskos, K., & Christies, J. (2001). On not pushing too hard: A few contrary remarks about linking literacy and play. *Young Children, 56*(3), 64–66.

Snow, C. E., Burns, S., & Griffin, P. (1998). *Preventing reading difficulties in young children.* Washington, DC: National Academy Press.

Children's Book Cited

Steig, W. (1971). *Amos and Boris.* New York: Farrar, Strauss, & Giroux.

Chapter 1

Children's First- and Second-Language Development

> Why they have straight ears?
> —Aliyah, a kindergartner, looking at a picture
> of a kangaroo in a book

TEACHING AND LEARNING QUESTIONS

1. What are important language-learning experiences for infants, toddlers, and preschoolers? And what are the implications for older children's language development?
2. What are critical factors for children in learning a second language? What challenges do English-language learners face and what are their resources?
3. How can we make connections for children between their first- and second-language learning?
4. What is the role of teachers and families in the process of language learning in school, home, and community?

FIRST-LANGUAGE DEVELOPMENT

The potential for successful language and literacy experiences for preschool and primary-grade children are grounded in their earliest language experiences as newborns, infants, and toddlers. Their first movements, their babbling, cooing, and speaking words are precursors of their later language and literacy learning. It is helpful for those of us who teach preschool and the primary grades to take a glimpse back at children's earliest language learning, and to re-see and re-hear children's earliest explorations with using language to understand and experience their emerging worlds. It is also helpful to see and remember how unconscious and experientially based language use and learning is for children between the ages of birth and 3 years old, and how valuable this is as a reminder for those of us who work with older children and feel pressed to make language learning a highly conscious process and related more to paper-and-pencil work than to objects and experiences.

Earliest Language Experiences

Light, Objects, and Sounds

Newborns just days and a few weeks old are busy adjusting to the new experiences of day and night, of lightness and darkness. They struggle to adjust their eyes, minds, and senses to a new kind of experience with light. For example, when Kaili, my daughter, was just several days old, if I moved a curtain in a room that suddenly let in a splash of sunshine, Kaili would move her eyes to the source of new light. If the sunshine continued to be bright, Kaili would try to avert her eyes, as the light was too strong for her still adjusting eyes. These kinds of experiences with light consume most of the energy and attention of newborns and infants; they are learning to detect shades and degrees of darkness and lightness, learning to discern the basic patterns of light. (Older children, those learning to read and write, are learning to discern the black squiggles on the written page against the white backdrop of the paper. They are learning to detect basic patterns in the shapes and sounds of letters, words, phrases, sentences.)

Newborns and infants also encounter the wholly new world of movement and objects. At 3–4 months old, Kaili delighted in twirling one of her hands slowly, mesmerized by its movement and the motion. She was discovering a part of her body and seeing what it could do; the motions were pleasing, and she spent long periods of time gently moving her hands with the utmost fascination. A little later on, Kaili moved her fingers, too, and enjoyed watching others rhythmically move their fingers and hands in front of her.

At several months of age, infants pay attention to the pointing gestures of adults and older children. They seem to recognize this nonverbal activity as particularly important to pay attention to, especially when adults repeatedly ask for their attention by pointing and gesturing. At first, infants simply look at the finger or arm of the person pointing (or the person him- or herself) and not at the object or place being pointed to. For example, when I pointed to a ball that had rolled away from Kaili, she looked at my hand and index finger rather than toward the ball. Over time, as infants develop their linguistic, cognitive, and social skills, they orchestrate their ability to fixate on an object indicated by a gesture or pointing.

Newborns and infants delight in the discovery of their first sounds. As anyone with experience with newborns can attest to, they often have a healthy set of lungs, and can cry for long periods of time and at a rather high decibel level. Some of their early sounds include sighing, crying, yawning, and high cat-like sounds as they experiment with their nascent abilities to produce sound. As their vocal apparatus develops in sophistication through changes in physical structure, their repertoire of sounds also grows. Infants between 2 and 6 months move on to gurgling, babbling, and cooing and of course continue to cry. Some infants toward the later stage of this period believe they are budding opera singers; Kaili sat in her small bouncer chair in the kitchen and repeatedly produced high and loud operatic arias, and was particularly pleased with this attention-getting achievement. Newborns and infants also love music boxes, songs, humming, music from the record player, objects that make noise such as baby rattles, and any kind of handmade or commercial noise-making object. They pay particular attention to melodies and sounds that are soothing and pleasant to their ears. The rhythmic, constant shaking of a rattle or the soft humming of an adult's voice are interesting and calming.

Turn-Taking, Conversation, and the Role of Play

Newborns and infants engage in turn-taking and exchanges of sounds and movement with their families and other caretakers. In this process, newborns and infants gain valuable experience in mimicking, repeating, adapting, and complementing others in their immediate social worlds. The turn-taking involves a variety of nonverbal and verbal interaction. For instance, breast and bottle feeding are examples of primarily nonverbal turn-taking. In this process, newborns and adults often exchange nonverbal glances, smiling back and forth or opening their eyes wide back and forth in turn-taking fashion. Oral language can be part of this experience, too, as newborns and infants gurgle, coo, and babble and adults echo these sounds or talk. In countless instances, infants and adults experience a back-and-forth of nonverbal and oral language that form infants' earliest turn-taking experiences.

Newborns start off life playful, grasping an object such as a finger or a rattle, eager to experiment with manipulating anything that is within reach. As they develop their fine- and gross-motor skills, they expand the horizon of possibilities for play and seek out playful objects and situations. Infants continue their interest as newborns in manipulating small objects and in moving their fingers and hands, and transfer these interests to other objects in playful ways. For example, at around 10 months of age, Kaili would hold on to a low bookshelf and fling book after book behind her on to the carpet. As she tossed the books, Kaili made little sounds to accompany her actions. At first, my wife and I thought, "Oh no, the books are getting ruined." But the books weren't damaged. We joined in the turn-taking aspect of the activity, turning it into a playful game, by placing the books back on the shelf so Kaili could start her book-flinging all over again.

What are Kaili and other infants learning about language through this kind of play? As the Russian psychologist Lev Vygotsky believed, since play is ahead of development, when young children engage in language play they are experimenting with new and more sophisticated levels of language understanding and use. Kaili, for example, gained the experience of repeating a single action (tossing the books) over and over again; this provided her with the experience of repeatedly performing a pleasing action. Second, Kaili learned that a certain area of the environment (the bookshelf) can be a source of active experimentation and a playful game. Third, her delight in making sounds to accompany her book-flinging showed the interest of infants to connect their beginning sounds with their playful actions. Fourth, Kaili's repeated playfulness with the books invited nonverbal and verbal conversation with others. She received lots of language in return: "Where are those books going?" "Oh no, don't fall." "Let me help you pick them up and put them back." "Let's put the books back so you can easily get them." "Let's pile up the books on the floor." "OK, now they are all back on the shelf."

First Words

Newborns and infants sense lightness and darkness, perform movements, make sounds, experience turn-taking, and play with objects and people. Typically, infants go on to say their first words between 12 and 18 months, and quickly gather steam after that as they build a spoken word vocabulary that grows with exposure, practice, and exploration. Before this period of active language development, newborns and infants gain valuable experience through simply listening and absorbing the verbal and nonverbal language of others. For example, at some point if an adult says, "Can you go and pick up your big red ball?" an infant will crawl or walk off the living-room rug and pick up a ball lying under the dining-room table. The infant understands the linguistic intent even if the adult does not gesture or point to the ball. He or she has a sense and understanding now for words (*ball*) and phrases (*your big red ball*) that enable interaction with other children and adults and engagement in increasingly sophisticated actions.

Often around the same age, infants start saying words that we recognize. Many children will also continue to babble, make spontaneous playful sounds, and say words that we don't recognize as conventional or "real." These made-up words often sound quite similar in sound and pronunciation to words in the languages that children hear and that we speak. For the past year or so, infants have been acutely aware of the rhythm, cadence, pitch, and feel of the languages close to home, and they are now ready to mimic and produce some of these aspects of language on their own.

Between the ages of 1 and 2 years, children's spoken vocabulary increases rapidly. They are interested in and learn a rich variety of words associated with people, actions, situations, objects, and play and social situations. For example, the vocabulary of Michael, an English-speaking 19-month-old, integrated important elements and people in his immediate environment:

Names: Mama, Dada, Joe
Objects: ball, more (his pacifier), baba (baby), truck, mouse (for Mickey Mouse), block, bow (hair bow), hat, sock, shoe, fork, book, house, light, duck, bubbles, plate, chalk
Actions: jump, hugs, hide, slide, hi, bye-bye, bite, kick, roll

Food: juice, cookie, milk, cheese
Body Parts: head, nose, mouth, eye, belly
Animal Noises: meow, woof, quack, monkey noises, jump (frog), roar
Social Situations: three, gum (thank you), mine, yes, no, uh-uh (yes),
     all gone, up, up (open), sorry

While not all children of this age will have this same vocabulary, it does indicate the range of possible word categories for young children.

The Routines of Daily Life

Much of children's earliest language occurs within the daily routines of eating, sleeping, playing, bathing, walking, going to the park, getting in the car, going on the bus, reading books, listening to music, singing. At around 2 years of age, Kaili delighted in saying and hearing the names of the children and adults she knew and saw on a fairly regular basis. Before she went to sleep, she loved to say a long string of names. I would start off the game by saying, "Let's say goodnight to . . ." Kaili completed the phrase by saying, "Jim, Debbie, Linda, Lee," the names of our neighbors. In a variation of this playful name game, I'd say, "Good night, Cody" (her cousin) and Kaili would repeat, "Good night, Cody." Or sometimes Kaili initiated the routine by saying, "Good night, Cody" and then I repeated "Good night, Cody." Another variation of this routine involved Kaili or another adult saying someone's name, and then Kaili liked to list the other children or adults associated with that person. If I said, "Hartley" (her friend), Kaili would reply, "Hartley, Peter [his father], Lucinda [his mother]."

As children of this age gain proficiency and fluency with single words, they begin to produce two- and three-word strings that are sometimes attached to "nonsense" words that make for a longer sentence. Young and older toddlers are eager to string their words together into longer chunks of language. For example, at 19 months, Kaili first learned to say "Anya" and then "house" whenever we passed Anya's house on our walks. Later on, Kaili said, "Anya house" and pointed to the house when we walked by. She began to transfer this two-word skill to other people on our street: "Mick house," "Linda house," "Rio [neighbor's dog] house." Around the same time, Kaili learned to say, "I want to . . ." and then point to something she wanted to do or have. "What is that?" was another favorite phrase. "What is that?" can go a very long way in terms of holding a conversation with an adult, as toddlers endlessly point to objects.

In this process of children's first attempts at identifying and describing their environment through words, adults (and older children, too) are important listeners and conversational partners. Adults extend and stretch both the meaning and the form of children's earliest words and word combinations. For example, adults can stretch language, as in this example of a dialogue with a 23-month-old child:

JANET: Janet doing?
ADULT: What *is* Janet doing?
JANET: Janet bubbles.
ADULT: Janet is blowing bubbles.

The adult extended the child's phrase through intonation and emphasis ("What *is* Janet doing?") and more words ("Janet is blowing bubbles").

Adults can also extend and elaborate children's language use during such routine group and social times as snack or lunch. In the following example, the teacher talks with her group of 2-year-old toddlers during snack time:

ARTHUR: I went airport.
TEACHER: You went to the airport.
SPENCER: Yeah.
TEACHER: What did you see at the airport?
SPENCER: Um, lights.
TEACHER: Lights.
SPENCER: Yeah, Jeffra go too [stops, looks around].
TEACHER: Jeffra went with you to the airport.
ARTHUR: Yeah.
ANN: [Another child joining in] Well, I saw light too with my sister and
     my momma.
TEACHER: With your sister and your momma you saw the lights? What
     else did you see?
ANN: I saw food coming.
TEACHER: You saw food coming.
ANN: At the airport.
JOHNNY: Food in the shape of a snowman.

Through simple repetition and a little questioning, the teacher keeps the "language ball" rolling, extending children's language and encouraging other children—who weren't even at the airport—to join in.

Stories

Stories are powerful vehicles for understanding and articulating children's knowledge and interests. In the following example, 6-year-old Valeria's dictated story indicates children's early sophistication with story.

Once upon a time there was a little girl. She wanted to go in the cave, but her mom said, "Don't go in the cave because there's some bears and they might eat you." And the little girl said, "Mom, they're not going to eat me." "Yes, they are." And then the little girl said, "I'm going to go play

outside." And her mom said, "OK, but don't go in the cave."
She said, "No, mom. I'm not going to go the cave." And then
she went to the cave, and she walked in there and the bears
eat her. The End.

Valeria's story contains fairy tale language ("once upon a time"), characters ("little girl," "mom," "bears"), setting ("cave"), intention ("she wanted
to go in the cave"), a potential problem ("but don't go in the cave . . ."), a
quite dramatic ending ("she walked in there and the bears eat her"), and
an implied moral (always listen to your mother).

Children are also capable of retelling stories they have heard or read
in books. Five-year-old Jason delighted in retelling part of the Jack and the
Beanstalk story:

> Jack said, "Hi Mom, these are some magic beans" and then
> [Mom says] "You got magic beans?" [Jack says] "from this
> old lady." [Mom replies] "Uh, you got some magic beans
> from this old lady?" And then he said, "Jack you're bad, go
> to your bed!" And then his mom threw the beans out of the
> window and then when he woke up he saw a big giant bean
> sack.

Like Valeria's story, Jason's narrative contains storybook language ("magic
beans"), dialogue ("You got magic beans?"), phrases ("big giant bean sack"),
long sentences with multiple actions and events ("his mom threw the beans
out of the window and then when he woke up he saw a big giant bean
sack"), and connectives to keep the story going ("and," "and then").

Storytelling with children provides sophisticated models of gesture,
inflection, vocabulary, syntax, character, plot, and cultural traditions. I know
a wonderful professional storyteller, Muriel Johnson, who retells a story
called "Sody Sallyratus" (see Teri Sloat's *Sody Sallyratus*, 1997) in which
a big scary bear eats several characters in search of baking soda ("sody
sallyratus") for making hot buttered biscuits. Young children gain experience of certain literary techniques as the story progresses. For instance, at
one point Muriel pauses and says, "Meanwhile back at home . . . ," and
children are asked to hold momentarily what has just gone in the story,
switch to a new setting, and then anticipate a return to the main story line
a short while later. Stories, as told with such a superb sense of developmental and cultural responsiveness, foster a memory for favored tales, favored
characters, and twists of plot.

Language Components

Through conversation, story, and play, young children from infancy
to the primary grades develop their phonological (language sounds), syn-

tactical (word order), semantic (word meaning), and pragmatic (language use in social situations) capabilities for language.

Phonology

Phonological development is important for infants and toddlers who are learning their first words and older children learning to read and write. Infants and toddlers, eager to hear and pronounce words for the first time, listen for the unique sounds to distinguish words, learning to recognize their rhythm and to articulate the sounds. This often means a "close-enough" approximation of a word. For example, as a toddler, Kaili said "noonoo" for *noodles*, "buhbuh" for *bubble*, "beeh bowl" for *big ball*, "awt" for *hot*, "suhlsuh" for *salsa*, and "allo" for *hello*. In other instances, children's first words approximate the sounds and/or actions of an object. For example, Kaili said "choo choo" for train, "wuff wuff" for our neighbor's dog, "boom" or "I go boom" for the action of falling down, "ow" or "owee" for the action of getting hurt, and "ow" for "meow" to identify a cat. In another example, Andrew, a 32-month-old child, first began to call out for his caregiver, Evangeline, by saying "Hi Da!" This progressed a few weeks later to "Hi dandin!" then to "Hi Dandelin," and finally to "Hi Vangelynn" one month later.

Syntax

In terms of syntactical development, young children learn to understand and produce more sophisticated phrases and sentences. For instance, 3-year-old Anna exhibited a range of syntactical learning over the course of a 3-month period, as indicated by the following list chronicling her development:

1. Come on. [Talking to her friend Jenny about running to a hill]
2. Jessica, I went to zoo. [Told to her teacher Jessica a few weeks after Anna went to the zoo]
3. Jessica, my mommy take me to zoo. I saw iguana.
4. Jessica, Jessica, mommy take me to zoo. I saw a baby bear. The baby bear was sleeping. I saw a giraffe and he eat like [stretches her neck out as she tells the group of children in class one month after visiting the zoo].
5. I went to Alejandro's birthday. My daddy take me to Alejandro house. We had cake. Yum cake. I have birthday. You come to my birthday, Jessica. Come to my house. [Told to Jessica after Alejandro's birthday]

In the short span of 3 months, Anna extended her command of word order in English as she puts words together into word strings, lengthens her sentences, and alters sentence structure.

Semantics

Over time, young children acquire an increasingly large and sophisticated vocabulary for conversing with others, exploring their environment, and initiating their own behavior, thoughts, and feelings. Toddlers and preschoolers are often quite insistent in asking for information and reasons. "Why is that, Mommy?" And then once they hear an answer, they ask again, "But why?" Preschoolers and kindergarten-age children love riddles and jokes, as they delight in playing on the real and intended word meanings.

In Kaitlin's kindergarten class, the children learned to make paper and then brainstormed a list titled "Ways We Can Describe Paper."

soggy	rough	bumpy	smooth	hard
fluffy	puffy	stretchy	colorful	flat
bent	sticky	wet	scrunchy	skinny
fat	soft	shiny	three-dimensional	

In another project, on mathematical shapes, the children created a list of words titled "What We Know About Our Shapes."

Sphere	*Cube*	*Cone*
ancestor of a circle	8 corners	1 point
no corners	6 squares	1 circle
balls	dice	flat
bounce	house or building	it's a triangle
roll	clubhouse	
throw it	blockheads	

The following year, in first grade with the same children, Kaitlin continued the focus on understanding word meanings within the larger context of a project. The children studied architecture, reading books about architectural forms, taking neighborhood walks to look at architectural features, composing a word wall of architectural terms, building their own miniature homes, and dictating descriptions of their houses:

JONAH: My house has stairs. My house has a door. It has a gargoyle that looks a little like a snake. It has windows of course. It has a backyard too. It's very colorful and it's on stilts. On the back it's all black and there's a window in the back of the house too.

MARIA: My house is a big, long house. It has the address of my real
house. There is a blue gargoyle on my house and purple paintings
of oils on the side. My house has double doors, eaves, and window
sills. The windows have curtains for the little boy's room and the
little girl's room. There's a balcony which is hard to see. I like my
house because it is very old.

ARTHUR: My house has a crystal that's lighted by the sun. It has all the
colors of the rainbow. On the front and back door there is a key-
stone. It has windows and arches and stairs. My house is surrounded by nature.

Pragmatics

Pragmatic language refers to language used in social situations. Children experience aspects of pragmatic language use in a range of social and
learning contexts—everything from an infant learning to take turns passing
a rattle back and forth while smiling, to a 3-year-old talking with her older
sister while eating breakfast, to a 6-year-old answering a teacher's question
during circle time. Pragmatics also includes such socially expected language
as *please* and *thank you*, culturally influenced forms of social address and
greetings (honorific titles for grandmother or grandfather), and nonverbal
communication such as bowing, hugging, kissing, and making eye contact.
When Kaili was a toddler, she loved to walk around (even if no one was in
her way), saying, "Shooz me, shooz me, shooz me."

Friends and other children influence children's use of language
in social situations. For example, the start-of-school greetings between
3-year-olds Anna, Jenny, and Irma helped them become friends over a
period of time. The following examples are listed in chronological order
over 3 months.

ANNA'S GREETINGS

ANNA: [To Jenny] Hi. Come on. Go hill? [Go up the hill together]
ANNA: Come on. Jenny let go find Irma. Bye daddy.
ANNA: Jeanette. I went to the zoo and saw iguana.

JENNY'S GREETINGS

JENNY: Hi Anna.
JENNY: Hi Anna. OK bye Daddy.

IRMA'S GREETINGS

IRMA: Hi Anna.
IRMA: Hi Anna, Jenny. Irma play?

The children use words of greeting to initiate socially acceptable forms of friendship and play.

Putting It All Together

Phonology, syntax, semantics, pragmatics—when adults help children "to put it all together" they gain critical experiences in using language to learn about their world. In the following example from Kaitlin's kindergarten classroom, the children interviewed Rachel, the school's gardening teacher, as part of their year-long gardening project.

ANGEL: Where did you grow up?
RACHEL: I grew up in Los Angeles, California.
MARIAH: How old were you when you first started gardening?
RACHEL: I learned from my mother when I was 8 years old.
DANIEL: When did you start learning about flowers and seeds?
RACHEL: I learned by going out into nature. My dad took us on walks. I watched the soil.
JOHNNY: How did you plant the garden at our school?
RACHEL: I called people to help. I got lumber from stores for wood. I organized a work party for Earth Day.
DANTE: What do you plant in the garden?
RACHEL: We plant collard greens, beets, chard, kale, and other things to eat.
ANNIE: When did you grow carrots and tomatoes?
RACHEL: We grew carrots and tomatoes 3 years ago and tomatoes this year.

Articulating words such as *tomatoes* and *carrots*, the children indicate their phonological abilities. In asking questions such as "How did you plant the garden at school?" the children understand the form of a question and use the correct syntactical order. In thinking of questions to ask Rachel, the children show an understanding of word meanings. In asking questions and listening to the responses, the children indicate an understanding of the pragmatic aspects of an interview.

Young children 0–6 years of age are learning a tremendous amount of language at a rapid pace. They absorb and internalize the forms of oral and nonverbal language that surround them, and take an active role in producing, performing, and exhibiting their language growth for themselves and for others. In this process, young children learn to remember critical elements of effective communication and expression and learn to commit to memory those aspects of language that begin to define themselves as individuals and as members of families and communities. In this sense, young children's earliest memories for sounds and words are those that are the most human and the most intimate. These are the sounds and words that we hear before we are born, as we are born, and as we learn to listen, to see, to grasp, to point, to walk, and to talk. It is this intimate foundation of language as internalized memory—in our hearts and in our minds—that children carry with them as they learn other languages.

SECOND-LANGUAGE DEVELOPMENT

Mr. Meier: Is learning English hard or easy? [Asked to Brenda, a Spanish/English bilingual preschooler]

Brenda: Hard. You have to repeat somebody. Spanish is easy; you have to repeat somebody, too.

Mr. Meier: Which language did you learn first?

Brenda: Spanish. Then the other one.

Mr. Meier: Which do you speak better? English or Spanish?

Brenda: Both of them.

First Words in a New Language

Second-language learning, as well as learning even a third or fourth language, has close parallels to children's first-language development. In terms of children's overall learning and growth, and their attachment to their cultural identity and families, maintaining a first language and learning a second language is a powerful journey. Children who are provided with home and school experiences in multilingual language use can become bilingual speakers and bicultural members of community and educational settings. However, if children are only hearing and using a new second language in the home and at school, it is likely that they will stop speaking their first language and adopt the new second language. This process can lead to a loss of cultural identity and the challenge of recovering the first language when children are older.

For second-language learning to become as long-lasting and intimate a process as learning to speak and use a first language, adults in home settings must create the same sense of closeness and power that young children experience in learning a first language. For instance, my wife spoke English and Tagalog (a primary language of the Philippines) to Kaili, my daughter, when she was an infant and toddler. Much of this second-language learning happened within Kaili's daily social interactions and play. As my wife moved a doll up and down in the air and said, *"Taas, baba"* (up, down), Kaili followed the up-and-down movement of the doll and listened to the rising intonation of *taas* and the following intonation of *baba*. Although Kaili could not say *taas* or *baba*, she experienced connecting the movement of objects with the sounds and rhythms of a new second language. In another example, when Kaili banged a toy or object too loudly, my wife would say, "*Dahan dahan*" (gently), as she repeated the words and showed Kaili how to gently use the toy or object. When Kaili made a parade out of her animals along the kitchen floor, my wife counted, "*Isa, dalawa, tatlo, apat, lima, anim, pito, walo, siam, sampo*" (1, 2, 3, 4, 5, 6, 7, 8, 9, 10) with Kaili.

Daily routines such as eating, bathing, and walking also help facilitate second-language learning. Kaili learned the names of body parts in Tagalog during her daily bath. In order to get Kaili's entire body washed, and also to learn more Tagalog, my wife made up a game of saying a body part in Tagalog and then letting Kaili point to the part—*ulo* (head), *paa* (foot), *kamay* (hand), *kili kili* (underarms), *pusod* (bellybutton). My wife stretched the game by asking Kaili, "*Asan ang paa*?" (Where is your foot?) and "*Asan ang kamay*?" (Where is your hand?), which made another game for the two of them to play.

Language Components

For older children, second-language learning continues to involve the process of mastering aspects of phonology, syntax, semantics, and pragmatics in a new language. In school settings, this process can become more challenging if children do not have access to their first language when they are learning how to read and write.

Phonology

In learning aspects of phonology in a new language, children experience all over again the journey of developing an ear for the particular rhythms and intonation of words in a language, a process that takes time, discovery, and practice. In learning English as a second language, there are particular aspects of the language that can pose special challenges for children. For instance, when I worked with Diana, a Spanish-speaking kindergartner, she said /jello/ for *yellow*, /sebra/ for *zebra*, /de/ for *the*, /be/ for the letter *b*. Han, a Korean-speaking kindergartner, said /huppa/ for *hippo*, /cahmeya/ for *camera*, /bananos/ for *bananas*. Both Diana and Han were giving very close approximations of these unfamiliar English words, trying hard to physically articulate the sounds they heard and to replicate the particular consonant and vowel sounds of English.

Syntax

Syntactical development, just as in children's first-language learning, plays a critical role in second-language learning. In learning English as a second-language, there are certain challenges for children, given the particular structure and organization of English. The following aspects of English syntax can prove challenging for English learners:

- The verb "to be" ("I am," "you are," "he/she/it is," "we are," "you [plural] are,"
- Subject-verb-object order ("He hit the ball")
- Prefixes and suffixes ("*mis*understand" and "stand*ing*" respectively)
- Adjectives preceding nouns ("red ball" and "small, low, white fence")
- Auxiliary verbs ("I have gone," "I won't drive," "I can't drive")

For example, Johnny, a Spanish-speaking kindergartner, said "cat with a purple" instead of "the purple cat" from *Brown Bear Brown Bear* by Bill Martin and Eric Carle. He knows from his first language, Spanish, that adjectives follow nouns, and is in the early stages of learning that this order is reversed in English.

In another example, when I read a book with Han and he tried to remember the text, he said "I am smile" instead of the text's "I am laughing," "I am sad" instead of "I am crying," "I am telephone" instead of "I am talking," and "I am sleep" instead of "I am sleeping." This example shows how Han is working toward correct or commonly accepted English word order and sentence structure. At the moment, the English *-ing* suffixes are a bit beyond Han, although he understands and uses the English subject-verb structure in "I am sleep."

In another instance, I read a book with Huma, an Urdu-speaking kindergartner, and wanted her to begin memorizing the new text pattern. I read the book first, pointing to the words and the pictures of the animal characters who go in and out of a bear's cave. The text uses the sentence pattern of "The _____ [animal] ran out." As we reread the text to commit it to memory, Huma kept saying "comes out" instead of "ran out." Huma had not quite mastered fine distinctions in English between present and past tense (*ran* in addition to *run*), and so used the present tense *comes* as her verb. This actually worked in terms of the overall meaning for the context—"The goat comes out" has essentially the same meaning as "The goat ran out"—but lacks the more refined and specific sense of the past tense *ran* as indicating the goat being scared by the bear.

Semantics

English learners use a variety of their own strategies for communicating as they try to learn words in a new language. One strategy is to postpone the challenge of speaking in English and simply talk in the first language with English speakers. For example, Neeral, a 3-year-old from India, speaks Gujarati to his peers and teachers at his preschool. A social child eager to play and be with others, Neeral shows no hesitation in the value and usefulness of speaking Gujarati in order to initiate and maintain social contact and to communicate. Over a period of several months, in which he continued to use Gujarati, Neeral also increased his understanding and use of English vocabulary with peers and his teachers.

English learners also use gestures and sound effects to approximate new word meanings in English. For example, Han and I were looking at a book and identifying objects in the pictures.

MR. MEIER: This is a picture of . . . ?
HAN: Tchk, tchk. [Han held up his fingers and made the sound that the chain makes when turning a light off] Sssss ssssss. [He then made a snoring sound as if he had just turned off the light and fallen asleep]
MR. MEIER: Yes, that's it. This is a picture of a light or lamp. You turn it off and on.

Han did not know the English word *lamp* or *light* to identify the picture, but he did know how a light functions and so used nonverbal language (turning off an imaginary light) and sound effects ("tchk tchk" to make the clinking sound of the light and "sss sssss" to indicate sleeping) to approximate the English word. Another time, we read a book with a picture of a bathtub.

MR. MEIER: Han, do you take a shower or a bath? [I pointed to the picture]
HAN: I do tsss tsss. [Han made the sound of falling water and put his head up as if standing under a shower]

In both instances, Han compensated for not knowing the exact English vocabulary by relying on what he knew from experience with the objects and his beginning knowledge of English.

Using new words in a second language also involves an understanding of the "sense," or subtle uses and meanings, of words. For example, Lupe, a Spanish-speaking kindergartner, and I were reading a book. Relying on her memory of the book's text pattern, and in looking at the pictures, Lupe read, "I am hearing" for the book's text of "I am listening." Lupe is technically correct—the girl in the book is hearing the person on the other end of the phone—but in terms of the sense of the scene, it is closer to "listening." In English, which has many words with somewhat similar meanings, *hearing* and *listening* are similar in meaning but are not always used in the same ways. It will take time—and lots of talking, reading, and writing—for Lupe to internalize the subtle distinctions.

In another example of learning the nuances of word meanings, Jesus, a Spanish-speaking kindergartner learning English, was identifying objects in a bag. The bag happened to contain (1) a plastic lid for a yoghurt container, (2) a small metal cap (pulled off) from a bottle of soda pop, and (3) a

slightly larger metal top (twist off) from a bottle of juice. I did not anticipate the variety of possible English words for these three common objects
when I put them in the bag, but Jesus soon revealed their complexity of
vocabulary. He called all three objects *tops*, which is essentially correct. Yet
there were subtleties of meaning that he missed; I explained that one was a
lid (for the yoghurt), one was called a *cap* (for the soda pop bottle), and the
third object was called a *top* (for the juice bottle).

Using Two or More Languages at Once

Children who are in varying stages of learning and using more than
one language may combine the different languages depending on the linguistic and social setting. This mixing can happen within a single sentence when
children insert a word or phrase from another language (code-mixing), and
it can also happen when children say one sentence or more in one language
and then switch to saying whole sentences in a different language (code-
switching). When children act as family translators, translating what a
teacher or another adult says, they often code-switch, talking with the
teacher in English and then speaking another language to their parent in
order to translate what their teacher said.

In some situations, young children are exposed to multilingualism
at a young age. For example, Diana, who is 26 months old, is learning more
than one language at once. Her parents speak to her in Chinese and English; her babysitter in Tagalog; her grandmother in Bicol (dialect from the
Philippines), Tagalog, and Chinese; and other family members in Tagalog,
English, and Chinese. In the following conversation, three languages—
Chinese, Tagalog, and English—are used with Diana.

MOTHER: Diana, *siob* ["come here" in Chinese], *ligo na tayo* ["let's take a
bath" in Tagalog]. *Tan-ne* ["later" in Chinese] *ka na maglaro* ["you
can play" in Tagalog], *chang diao cha ti-thoh* ["after you have taken
a bath you can play" in Chinese].
DIANA: Uhmm. (Diana doesn't get up to take the bath)
MOTHER: *Dali na, hindi ka ba sasama?* ["Hurry, aren't you going with us?"
in Tagalog]. We're going to the zoo later *kaya* ["so" in Tagalog] you
need to take a bath *na* ["already" in Tagalog].
DIANA: No. (Diana continues to play)

Each of the three languages used by Diana's mother conveys different inten-
tions and subtleties, and the combination of all three is intended to coax
Diana into her bath!

In an example of using more than one language in school, three preschoolers are playing at the play-dough table. Leilani and Nathalie speak
Spanish and are learning English, while Nyalah speaks only English.

LEILANI AND NATHALIE: Hi! (to Norma, their teacher, passing by)
NORMA: Hi, you three.
LEILANI: (turning to Nathalie) *Quiero ir afuera.* [I want to go outside.]
NATHALIE: *Yo tambien.* [Me, too.] (Both girls go outside; a few minutes
    later Nathalie comes back and talks to Nyalah) You want to go
    outside?
NYALAH: OK. (The girls run outside and join Leilani on the swing)

In another example, Lupita and Ana, two Spanish-speaking kindergartners
learning English, use English and Spanish as they play a game of Go Fish
with me.

ANA: My turn? Your turn. (To Lupita)
LUPITA: *Este turno?*
ANA: I got four. (I.e., four cards) Hey, give me. This is mine. (Wants two
    cards back from Lupita)
LUPITA: *Que pasó?*
ANA: *Nada,* nothing.

In my presence, Ana and Lupita try out English phrases that show posses-
sion ("I got four") and turn-taking ("My turn").
    Two other examples, both from a English/Japanese bilingual pre-
school, show how the use of a single word in a second language can have an
important function for children who are learning to speak in two languages.
In the following example, Toshio, a Japanese-speaking preschooler learning
English, is at the sink washing his hands as Kayoko, his teacher, walks in.

KAYOKO: *Oshiko ni itta?* [Did you go pee-pee?]
TOSHIO: *Toshio ne* try *shitakedo denakatta.* [I tried, but pee-pee did not
    come out.]
KAYOKO: *Honnto?* [Really?]
TOSHIO: *Honnoto dayo.* Try *shita yo.* [Yes, I tried.]

Toshio experiments with the English verb *try,* by inserting it in the middle
and at the beginning of two sentences. By only using one English word,
with the rest of the words in Japanese, he can rely on his Japanese as a stepping stone for learning more English.
    In another example, Soniki is in line at the bathroom and gets pushed
by another boy standing next to him.

SONIKI: *Sensei,* Danny *ga* push *shitayo.* [Teacher, Danny pushed me.]
KAYOKO: Did you push Soniki, Danny?
DANNY: No, I did because Soniki stepped on my foot first.
SONIKI: Soniki *wa* step *shitenaiyo.* [I did not step on his foot.]

In both instances of inserting English words (*try* and *push*), the children use a single English word to experiment with English while relying on their first language of Japanese with their teacher and peers.

Mixing two or more languages allows children with advanced bilingual language skills to participate in sophisticated language play and social interaction. The following two examples show how Erin, a 4-year-old who understands and speaks both English and Ilocano (a dialect from the Philippines), uses two languages to play with and have fun with her grandparents. In the first scene, Erin and her grandmother come home from a morning trip to the supermarket.

GRANDFATHER: *Ania't ginatang mo diay tienda?* [What did you buy at the store?]
ERIN: I don't know. (Shrugs her shoulders and repeats in Ilocano) *Diak amo "apo lakay."* [I don't know, Grandfather.]
GRANDFATHER: *Kasta.* [Good, like that] (Nods approvingly)
ERIN: (Laughs)
GRANDFATHER: *"Apo lakay" nga ruden nya.* [Just call me *apo lakay* from now on, OK.]
ERIN: *Haan ka na "tatang" en apo lakay en.* [You are no longer *tatang* (father), now you'll be known as *"apo lakay."*] (Jokingly)
GRANDFATHER: *Apo lakay an en.* (From now on I'll be *apo lakay*.)
ERIN: *Haan! Sika ti tatang ko.* (No! You're my *tatang*.)

Erin uses *apo lakay*, a term of respect for elders, in addressing her grandfather and uses English and Ilocano to tease and play with her grandfather verbally. Erin closes the exchange by informing her grandfather that she'll stick to her favorite name for him (*tatang*).

In the next example, Erin and her grandparents all switch back and forth between English and Ilocano in a spirited discussion on religion.

GRANDFATHER: *Nalipatam sa met ti ag loalon.* [I think you forgot how to pray.]
ERIN: In the name of the Father, the Son, and the Holy Spirit. Amen.
GRANDMOTHER: *Kasta, nya ti bagam ti apo?* [Good, like that. What do you want to ask God?]
ERIN: I wish I had a baby brother.
GRANDMOTHER: *Apo.* [God.]
ERIN: *Apo.*
GRANDFATHER: *Siak mut* wish *ko mut?* [What about my wish?] I wish that I had a lot of money.
ERIN: (Laughing) I wish *tatang* [grandfather] had a lot of money.
GRANDFATHER: *Ala.* [Oh, my gosh.] What about *nanang* [grandmother]?
ERIN: I wish *nanang* would buy me an accordion.

Again, Erin uses English and Ilocano to engage her grandparents in humorous, lively exchanges that bring them closer together socially.

Family and Community Support

As in the examples of Diana and her mother and of Erin and her grandparents, multilingual and bilingual language learning involves intimate social and cultural connections with others. This kind of multilingual learning often takes hard work and persistence by schools and families. Norma Villazana-Price, a Spanish/English bilingual early childhood educator, notes the challenges that teachers and families face in maintaining a language other than English in contemporary U.S. society and schools.

> It's hard to maintain a first language in the United States because of the dominance of English. This is even more evident in the older grades in school where English is emphasized more. Many parents, too, want their children to learn English so their children won't struggle like they did. I worry, too, that in the present climate of attention to literacy at younger and younger age levels, that the push for English will get even worse. If there is more emphasis on reading and writing in English, then there is less emphasis on maintaining and promoting the first language.

Maintaining and promoting multilingualism on the part of families takes time, effort, and determination. For instance, Adrian, at 2½ years old, speaks and understands Korean, English, and Spanish. His mother was born in Korea, moved to the United States as a teenager, and speaks both English and Korean with Adrian both at home and out in the community. Adrian's father, who is from Spain, speaks both Spanish and English with Adrian at home and in the community. In using these three languages, Adrian's parents speak enough Korean, English, and Spanish on a daily basis so that Adrian is getting lots of rich language input and support around daily routines and family and community activities. It is also probably helpful that Adrian can identify Korean with his mother and Spanish with his father, though his father understands some Korean and his mother can speak and understand a beginning level of Spanish. This kind of parental/family language crossover is also important for developing Adrian's multilingualism. Further enhancing his language learning, Adrian attends a Spanish-English bilingual preschool, where he experiences Spanish language input and Latino/Chicano culture with adults and children.

Exemplifying how this kind of early family and school support can develop multilingualism later on in older children, Mehrnush, an 8-year-old, speaks, reads, and writes in English, Spanish, and Farsi. From birth, Mehrnush was surrounded with English and Farsi—Mehrnush's father speaks Farsi and English, while her mother speaks English and understands Farsi. When Mehrnush's grandmother visits from Iran, she speaks only Farsi with Mehrnush. In school, Mehrnush has attended a Spanish-English dual-immersion program since kindergarten—as she told her parents, "I already know how to speak English, so I'd like to learn a new language." Now in third grade, Mehrnush is at age-level fluency and skill as a bilingual English-Spanish speaker, knowledgeable and comfortable in both languages and able to switch back and forth between the two in social and academic situations.

Putting It All Together

Orchestrating speaking and understanding multiple languages has many similarities to learning and using a first language with fluency and ease. Children make discoveries about and use their rapidly expanding knowledge about the phonological, syntactical, semantic, and pragmatic aspects of a new language. They integrate this knowledge into what they consciously and unconsciously know about language from their first-language use. They go through a period of adjustment as they take in the sounds and rhythms of the new language and see where they can hold on to and use their first language to make friends, play, and successfully participate in educational activities.

Often, children go through a series of steps as they move toward more comfortable and effective second-language use. Norma Villazana-Price, through her teaching, has found a series of stages that children often experience in learning a new language. The following examples focus on Spanish-speaking preschoolers who are learning English as a second language.

Stage 1: A Quiet Beginning

Children learning English begin by listening to words and phrases in the new language and matching words with gestures and other nonverbal communication, and thus start to understand simple words and ideas in English. Often children prefer to listen for extended periods of time before attempting to speak in a new language. Some children prefer to speak only Spanish with peers and adults, while other children will speak Spanish and attempt some English words. Four-year-old Michael, for instance, liked to watch children speaking English and then tried to imitate some of their words. Leilani liked to play and talk with other Spanish-speaking children and yet also joined groups of children speaking or listening to English. She liked to listen to stories in English, concentrating on the sounds and intonation of the English words and syntax. Leilani then liked to look at the books and try to say some words in English on her own. For children at this time, it is helpful for the teacher to

- Build relationships with the child and family
- Encourage use of the first language with peers and adults in play and through listening to books.

Stage 2: Limited Use of Second Language

According to their individual temperaments and interests, the Spanish-speaking children began approaching adults to engage them and talk in English. This most often happened when children were hurt on the playground or needed assistance, and they sought out an adult who spoke Spanish. If none were available, they would seek an adult who spoke English. The children and the English-speaking adult would engage in nonverbal communication involving pointing and gestures, and the adult asked questions in English to gain more information from the child. For children at this time, it is helpful for the teacher to

- Encourage play and interaction with other children who speak the second language
- Sing songs, read books, and provide dramatic play opportunities in the second language
- Have adults who speak the second language take on a larger role in meeting the child's needs

Stage 3: Selected Use of Second Language

Interactions involving both nonverbal communication and spoken English provide children with a springboard for seeking out English-speaking children with whom to play games and do activities. At this stage the children would more often join a story-reading group or play with an English-speaking neighbor in English at their table. In addition, they started to use short English phrases to get their needs met with peers and adults. For instance, Nathalie would say to a teacher, "Read book." Leilani said, "Me, too?" to children already on the tire swing on the playground. Michael said, "I want juice," to a teacher at snack time. This more advanced use of English in social situations helped the children who spoke Spanish to form closer friendships with English-speaking peers and to form close connections with the English-speaking teachers. For children at this stage, it is helpful for the teacher to

- Continue to use the child's first language
- Provide play activities that encourage first- and second-language use
- Continue to model second-language use

The process of learning a second language takes the creative, patient, and sensitive guidance of teachers and family members as well as opportunities for daily interactions in the new language with peers. The multilingual journeys of Diana, Han, Erin, Nathalie, Leilani, Michael, and others are full of countless experiences of listening and absorbing the sounds, rhythms, and words of new languages. It is a lifelong process of learning about languages at home, in the community, and at school and internalizing words and sounds and meanings in our hearts, minds, dreams, hopes, and ideas.

This is essentially a journey of memory—of experiencing languages out in the world of action and sound, and then simultaneously seeing and feeling language become an intimate part of how children think and feel and create. In this sense, children's language learning becomes part of their lived memories, part of their small memories-in-the-making as they initiate play (Leilani and Nathalie) or talk with their grandparents (Erin). If children are provided with supportive and creative opportunities for multiple-language use at home and school, young children's memories for multilingualism will begin to coalesce and take shape. Children will begin seeing themselves as powerful users and communicators in more than one language, and their memories for language will inspire new discoveries and new memories.

SUGGESTED ACTIVITIES

1. Write down or draw your personal experiences as a child learning your first language. What are some positive and negative memories? Consider how these have influenced your language and literacy teaching.
2. Write or draw your personal experiences as a child, an adult, or both, in learning a second or third language. What were critical factors and components that supported your multilingual learning? Circle those factors that you would like to add to your own teaching.
3. Consider one of the children in your class. Write a poem or a first-person narrative from the child's internal perspective–how he or she experiences learning a new language in your classroom. What does the child find easy? Hard? What are his or her fears and hopes?
4. Speak with the family of one of the English learners in your class. To what extent do adults want their child to learn English, and why? To what extent do the adults want their child to retain the home language, and how, where, and why? Then consider how you can incorporate this information into working with all the families of your students.
5. If you are an administrator, write down a list of critical areas in which you feel most comfortable helping your staff learn about children's language development. Then consider how you might plan a professional development course of study for a school year on children's multilingual learning.

USEFUL RESOURCES

First-Language Development

Beck, I. L., McKeown, M. G., & Kucan, L. (2003). Taking delight in words: Using oral language to build young children's vocabularies. *American Educator*, *27*(1), 36–41, 45–48.

Berk, L. E. (1994, November). Why children talk to themselves. *Scientific American*, 78–83.

de Boysson-Bardies, B. (1999). *How language comes to children: From birth to two years*. Cambridge, MA: MIT Press.

Golinkoff, R. M., & Hirsh-Pasek, K. (1999). *How babies talk*. New York: Dutton.

Koralek, D. (Ed.). (2003). *Spotlight on young children and oral language*. Washington, DC: National Association for the Education of Young Children.

Kratcoski, A. M., & Katz, K. B. (1998). Conversing with young language learners in the classroom. *Young Children*, 53(3), 30–33.

Lindfors, J. W. (1999). *Children's inquiry: Using language to make sense of the world*. New York: Teachers College Press.

Sandy, C. S., & Stout, N. S. (2002). Pillow talk: Fostering the emotional language needs of young learners. *Young Children*, 57(2), 20–25.

Tabors, O. (1998). What early childhood educators need to know: Developing effective programs for linguistically and culturally diverse kids and families. *Young Children*, 53(6), 31–42.

Vygotsky, L. S. (1978). *Mind in society*. Cambridge, MA: Harvard University Press.

Vygotsky, L. S. (1986). *Thought and language*. Cambridge, MA: MIT Press.

Stories and Narrative Development

Applebee, A. N. (1978). *The child's concept of story: Ages two to seventeen*. Chicago: University of Chicago Press.

Champion, T.B. (2003). *Understanding storytelling among African American children: A journey from Africa to America*. Mahwah, NJ: Lawrence Erlbaum.

Cook, J. W. (2001). Create and tell a story: Help young children who have psychological difficulties. *Young Children*, 56(1), 67–70.

Dyson, A. H., & Genishi, C. (Eds.). (1994). *The need for story: Cultural diversity in classroom and community*. Urbana, IL: National Council of Teachers of English.

Engel, S. (1995). *The stories children tell: Making sense of the narratives of childhood*. New York: W. H. Freeman.

Isbell, R. T. (2002). Telling and retelling stories: Learning language and literacy. *Young Children*, 57(2), 26–30.

Miller, P., & Sperry, L. (1988). Early talk about the past: The origins of conversational stories of personal experience. *Journal of Child Language*, (15), 293–315.

Nelson, K. (1989). *Narratives from the crib*. Cambridge, MA: Harvard University Press.

Paley, V. (1980). *Wally's stories*. Cambridge, MA: Harvard University Press.

Whaley, C. (2002). Meeting the diverse needs of children through storytelling. *Young Children*, 57(2), 31–35.

Bilingualism and Second-Language Acquisition

Baker, C. (2000). *A parents' and teachers' guide to bilingualism* (2nd ed.). London: Multilingual Matters.

Cummins, J. (1996). *Negotiating identities: Education for empowerment in a diverse society*. Ontario, CA: California Association for Bilingual Education.

Darder, A., Torres, R. D., & Gutíerrez, H. (Eds.). (1997). *Latinos and education: A critical reader*. New York: Routledge.

Fillmore, L. W. (1979). Individual differences in second language acquisition. In C. J. Fillmore, D. K. William, & S. Y. Wang (Eds.), *Individual differences in language ability and language behavior* (pp. 30–49). New York: Academic Press.

Fillmore, L. W. (1991). When learning a second language means losing the first. *Early Childhood Research Quarterly, 6*(3), 323–346.

Genesee, F. (Ed.). (1994). *Educating second language children: The whole child, the whole curriculum, the whole community*. New York: Cambridge University Press.

Genishi, C. (2002). Young English language learners: Resourceful in the classroom. *Young Children, 57*(4), 66–71.

Genishi, C., & Brainard, M. (1995). Assessment of bilingual children: A dilemma seeking solutions. In E. García & B. McLaughlin (Eds.), *Meeting the challenge of linguistic and cultural diversity in early childhood education* (pp. 49–63). New York: Teachers College Press.

Genishi, C., Yung-Chan, D., & Stires, S. (2000). Talking their way into print: English language learners in a prekindergarten classroom. In D. S. Strickland & L. M. Morrow (Eds.), *Beginning reading and writing* (pp. 66–80). New York: Teachers College Press.

Hakuta, K. (1986). *Mirror of language: The debate on bilingualism*. New York: Basic Books.

Krashen, S. (1985). *The input hypothesis*. Oxford, UK: Pergamon.

Krashen, S. (1999). *Condemned without a trial: Bogus arguments against bilingualism*. Portsmouth, NH: Heinemann.

Reyes, M. de la luz, & Halcon, J. (Eds.). (2001). *The best for our children: Critical perspectives on literacy for Latino children*. New York: Teachers College Press.

Tabors, P. (1997). *One child, two languages: A guide for preschool educators of children learning English as a second language*. Baltimore, MD: Paul H. Brooks.

Valdés, G. (2001). *Learning and not learning English: Latino students in American schools*. New York: Teachers College Press.

Children's Books Cited in Chapter

Martin, B., & Carle, E. (1967). *Brown bear, brown bear, What do you see?* New York: Holt, Rinehart & Winson.

Sloat, T. (1997). *Sody sallyratus*. New York: Penguin.

Chapter 2

Children's Early Literacy Development

I had just read Maurice Sendak's *Where the Wild Things Are* with a group of preschoolers.

Mr. Meier: How come when the boy came back from being away with the Wild Things, his dinner was "still hot"? How could that be?
Asante: Just before he got home, his mom warmed it up.
Julie: It didn't really happen at all; it was all just his imagination.
Gabe: His mom put hot sauce in it!

Teaching and Learning Questions

1. What are the literacy talents and resources of English-language learners? What literacy challenges do they face?
2. What is the relationship between children's language variety and early literacy learning?
3. What is involved in biliteracy, or learning to read and write in two languages?
4. What are the influential concepts and approaches related to teaching and learning in preschool and the primary grades? How can we use these for strengthening our understanding of children's early literacy learning?
5. What are useful ways of observing and assessing children's literacy learning? What is potentially problematic about literacy assessment?

CHILDREN'S RESOURCES FOR LITERACY LEARNING

Children's linguistic and cultural talents and resources are critical for their successful literacy learning. Educators who design and implement literacy and language arts programs that incorporate children's resources for literacy provide familiar and comfortable stepping stones for learning to read and write. This incorporation is especially important for children whose language and literacy experiences may not mirror literacy programs and expectations in our preschool and primary grade classrooms. For these children, we need to see and hear and understand their talents for literacy, and make changes in our literacy curriculum and teaching practices so children can make the most of their potential.

Language Variety: The "Englishes" We Speak and Use

In North America children speak and converse in varied forms of English (Englishes). For instance, some African American children may speak variations of the oral language forms and traditions that come under an umbrella of terms—Ebonics, Black English, Black English Vernacular, African American English, and Standard Black English. African American English is a time-honored, rich, sophisticated language with characteristics of phonology, syntax, semantics, and pragmatics that can vary from the Standard English traditionally emphasized in schools. In the following example, two African American preschoolers talk as they draw in their journals.

CHANTAL: Mr. Meier, look what I made! You all make this! (To the other
        children at the table)
LARRY: No. This is an egg [we had read Eric Carle's *The Very Hungry*
        Caterpillar]. It's going to pop up when the momma's gonna come
        out. I want this egg like this. (Points to a big circle he drew)
CHANTAL: That's a queen.
LARRY: I want a boy. Here's some space. I want another one like that!
CHANTAL: Look you all (to Larry and the two other children). Bet you
        can't do that (holds up her drawing).
LARRY: That funny! (Both Chantal and Larry laugh)

In the following conversation, two African American kindergartners talk as they write in their journals.

MICHAEL: There it go. There it is. (drawing a motorcycle)
EMILE: Is you playing with Kyla?
MICHAEL: No. Why did you want to know?
EMILE: Just wanted to know.

Elements of both conversations ("You all make this!" ". . . when the momma's gonna come out," "Look you all," "That funny," "There it go," "Is you playing with Kyla?") follow rule-governed, linguistic patterns in African American English oral language that communicate meaning, intention, and information just as effectively and powerfully as Standard English. The conversation also reveals how speakers of African American English combine and go back and forth between varied forms of English (from "That's a queen" to "that funny" and from "There it go" to "There it is") with skill, familiarity, and communicative power.

    Children's use of African American English can have certain important implications for literacy learning. Children's dictation and oral reading are two instances where we can put into practice our understanding of the range of Englishes involved in early literacy. In helping children link oral and written language, Alonzo Williams, a kindergarten teacher, emphasizes the overall goal of celebrating and extending children's Englishes.

> We need to validate languages, both the languages of the school and the languages of the home. I explain to children the appropriate environments for using certain languages. In school, we're teaching Standard English. This is important and critical for us as teachers to point out. For my students, I do connect African American English and Standard English. If we're explicit about how we approach it, and how our children speak in different ways, then that will help us teach our children. For instance in our interactive writing (done as a whole-group as the children themselves dictate and write on one large sheet of paper), I give my children a lot of power to use their languages as the foundation for our writing. In our journals, I do not want the children stuck on correctness; I want them to produce and be motivated. I provide mini-lessons on English language structure and conventions, and when I write in their journals, I always ask the children's permissions first. I then write down the spellings correctly, often saying something like, "You got the 'h' and the 's' and now you need the 'o, u, e' to make 'house.'" I don't focus on errors. I focus on making bridges to conventional written English in direct ways.

In an example of children's oral language influencing their oral reading, Michael, a kindergartner who speaks African American English and Standard English, and I were reading a book with this text: "I went to the shop. I looked in the window. I had no money." Michael was in the developmental stage of memorizing the text, using the pictures for clues, and actually reading a few simple words, but not at the point at which he could completely read and decode this much text. When we got to the line, "I had no money," Michael said, "I don't have no money." This reading makes perfect sense in terms of understanding the meaning of the sentence, and so I tell this to children (other children have read the text's sentence as "I ain't got no money" or "I don't got no money"). All three of these responses actually sound more lively, and more vividly express the possible frustration of the character in the story who is gazing forlornly into a toy store and knows he has no money! I tell children that "I don't have no money" is right and makes sense because that is the reality of the situation depicted in the book. I also tell children that there are other ways to read this situation, and that the sentence in the book actually reads, "I had no money." Children usually simply repeat this sentence, easily switching between the interrelated and yet distinct forms and constructions of Standard English (though the book is actually published in New Zealand) and African American English.

As teachers we can become familiar, if we aren't already, with the sound patterns, meanings, and constructions of African American English and help children navigate toward mastery of the range of possible Englishes. There are several philosophies and strategies that support the language and literacy talents of African American children:

- Use high-quality children's literature that depicts children's languages and varieties of English and experiences with power and authenticity (*Example*: using books by and about African Americans that depict characters, themes, experiences, and language forms relevant to the history of African American life in the United States and abroad)
- Structure small- and whole-group discussions and instructional time so that children can participate in a variety of ways (*Example*: structuring circle time or read-aloud time to include "quiet hand raising," call and response as a group, and spontaneous participation without hand raising)
- Refrain from correcting errors in children's oral language (*Example*: promoting meaning and intention over grammatical differences, as in not correcting Michael's question, "What kind a noise they make?" as he looks at a picture of baby lambs)
- Emphasize cooperation and collaboration for the general good of the whole group (*Example*: encouraging children to take one another's dictation rather than just the teacher acting as dictation scribe)
- Provide daily opportunities for children to talk and interact as they work and play (*Example*: promoting "space" for children's out-of-school ways of talking)
- Break down language and literacy instruction so children can see and learn the various forms of Standard English (*Example*: in taking children's dictation, point out the connections between "Mia and me, we be playin all day" and "Mia and I were playing all day.")

In these and many other ways, we honor and validate African American English speakers, readers, and writers and connect their talents and traditions with other Englishes in classroom settings. For the languages and Englishes that children bring to school are really the very same ones they need to carry away with them at the end of a school day that is filled with reading, writing, talking, and listening activities.

English-Language Learners

For English-language learners, much of the journey in learning to read and write in English parallels learning to understand and speak English.

Children learning to read and write in English also benefit from principles and strategies that promote first and second oral language development:

- Use of visuals and graphics
- Careful introduction and teaching of key vocabulary
- High-quality multilingual and multicultural children's literature
- Variety of books and texts that play on English sounds and rhythms
- Small doses of repetition and practice with English syntax and grammar
- Lack of error correction of English pronunciation and usage
- Informal attention to patterns and regularities in English spelling
- Rich and varied daily opportunities for talking and interacting with peers
- Use of concrete objects and hands-on literacy activities
- Incorporation of art and drama as well as other arts in literacy activities

Read-alouds, in which teachers read high-quality literature to children, are a particularly valuable activity for English-language learners. Marianne Geronimo, a primary-grade teacher, recommends the following for read-alouds, particularly with English-language learners:

- Use the primary language in reading and discussion. Hearing and using their first language provides children with a sense of comfort.
- Give children a choice when it comes to deciding which books to read out loud to them. Allowing children to choose some books maintains their interest.
- Know the story well. This will foster expression and character development when a book is read aloud. Reading an unfamiliar book usually results in a loss of fluency.
- Be enthusiastic. Children sense our moods, and if we are excited about a book, so will the children.
- Be consistent. Set aside a time of day when read-alouds will occur and stick with it. Knowing that they will have this time helps children look forward to it.
- Talk about the book. Children need follow-up discussions to facilitate comprehension.
- Know when to quit. Children, like us, are only interested for so long.

Biliteracy and Multiliteracy

In bilingual programs in preschools and primary-grade classrooms, the majority, if not all, of the children speak the same first language (such as Spanish) and are in the developmental process of acquiring a second language (for instance, English) in order to become proficient bilinguals. In dual or two-way language-immersion programs, the children often speak one or more of the languages (half may speak Spanish and half may speak English), and the language of the classroom in the early years is often in Spanish and then English is gradually introduced over time. Again, the ultimate goal is Spanish/English bilingual proficiency and fluency for both native Spanish speakers and native English speakers. Both of these language learning models may include children who are already well on the way toward bilingualism, having been exposed to a rich language environment and interaction in both Spanish and English from birth. So when they arrive in a preschool or kindergarten program, they already have access to language comprehension and production in two languages.

Given the large range of factors influencing this process of the development of biliteracy and multiliteracy, children do not attain reading and writing accuracy and fluency in more than one language at similar rates or in similar ways. There are a number of scenarios. For instance, if children are exposed to more than one language from a quite early age at home, they may well be interested in and capable of understanding and interacting with multilingual books upon entering preschool. For these bilingual and multilingual children, school experiences can have a powerful influence on fostering their biliteracy. We can capitalize, then, on children's bilingual oral language abilities as we introduce and guide children's biliteracy involvement. In this way, children's knowledge and language use transfers or carries over to learning to read and write in more than one language. Their memories for languages and literacies become compounded. Mehrnush is a child learning to read and write in English, Spanish, and Farsi. Her journey as that of an 8-year-old toward triliteracy is founded upon her oral language capabilities in the three languages—all fostered from an early age by home, community, and school.

Literacy Strategies

Literacy collaboration refers to instances in which children and adults increase each other's understanding of some aspect of learning to read and write. A child working independently can also develop strategies for literacy learning.

1. *Self-strategies.* Antwawn, a kindergartner, and I were retelling Eric Carle and Bill Martin's *Brown Bear Brown Bear, What Do You See?* with felt animals and the animal names written on cards. Antwawn put out the felt animals, and then I gave him each animal name card, which he placed by the relevant animal. In order to match the name cards with the animals, Antwawn created the strategy of repeating the name of each animal—"Brown bear, white dog, yellow duck"—each time we introduced a new animal. This was his way of adding to his own memory for matching the animals and name cards.

2. *Peer-to-Peer Collaboration.* Miguel, a Spanish-speaking kindergartner, and I read simple books in both English and Spanish. We read a book that used *hola* (hello) on almost every page to welcome a new animal: "hola tortuga," "hola jirafa," "hola cocodrilo," "hola oso," until "hola niña!" Jasmine, an English speaker who knew no Spanish but who was eager to befriend Miguel, happened to walk by. She spontaneously joined in by reading "*hola*" on each page, and Miguel finished the sentence by reading the Spanish words for the animals. Both Jasmine and Miguel delighted in their peer-to-peer collaboration, and Jasmine said, "Even though Miguel screams in my ear [in Spanish, presumably so she can understand him], he's my best friend." Although Miguel knew hardly any English, Jasmine claimed, "He be talkin English."

3. *Adult-to-Child Scaffolding.* Adult scaffolding of a literacy experience for children often works best when we revisit a book or activity over a period of time. The first time that I read Paul and Henrietta Strickland's *Dinosaur Roar!* I read the text and point to each dinosaur in the pictures. I also explain some of the vocabulary ("meek" and "fierce") through words, facial expressions, and gestures. The next few times that I read the book, I let the children identify the dinosaur that is "meek" or "fierce" or "sweet." Then, after several readings, the children have committed the text, pictures, and vocabulary to memory, and they can "read" and discuss the book all on their own. This process of breaking down a book—into its text patterns, vocabulary, message, and illustrations—over several readings helps English-language learners take their time absorbing and understanding the book's components.

Families

Families can provide us with valuable knowledge to tailor and adapt literacy curriculum to incorporate particular cultural and linguistic traditions and expectations for their children's literacy development. Through family surveys, classroom potlucks, and informal conversations, we can find out about families' literacy experiences and expectations regarding

- Family participation (how much time, energy, and resources can families give to their children's classroom?)
- Perspectives regarding the amount of play (how much time should be spent in the playhouse, block-building, art, movement?)
- Indirect versus direct literacy instruction (how important are opportunities for children to informally browse and "read" books versus teacher-directed instruction on how to read and decode text?)
- Content and images presented in children's literature and other literacy materials (how important are books with images that mirror the children's cultural backgrounds?)
- Amount and level of homework (are worksheets or reading at home or parent-child projects preferred?)

- English-language learners (what kind of support is preferred?)
- Bilingualism and biliteracy (is a bilingual/biliteracy program preferred?)
- Assessment and testing (what are opinions on formal, standardized tests?)
- Gender equity (how important is equal access for boys and girls in literacy activities?)
- Technology (how important is access to computers and other technology?)

In a complementary way, we can communicate our own views regarding these very same issues to families. This provides a two-way path of information and knowledge about literacy instruction for both teachers and families. We can then envision and implement a responsive and inclusive literacy program.

Memories for literacy—for words, ideas, books, discussions, reading, writing—are founded upon children's interests, talents, and resources. Powerful school literacy acknowledges and builds upon the range of Englishes that children bring to school, and that they carry home with them at the end of the day. Successful school literacy also supports the talents and needs of English-language learners and incorporates the expectations and hopes of families. It is in this process of collaboration and scaffolding of our teacherly ideas for literacy, children's language experiences, and families' hopes that we foster lifelong memories for literacy.

CONCEPTS AND APPROACHES RELATED TO EARLY CHILDHOOD TEACHING AND LEARNING

There are a number of concepts and approaches to teaching that have important implications for young children's language and literacy learning. First I will focus on two complementary concepts—developmentally appropriate practice and culturally responsive teaching. Then I will introduce three out of the many approaches to teaching in early childhood education. I have found the Montessori, Project, and Reggio Emilia approaches particularly relevant to language and literacy learning. (The "Useful Resources" at the close of this chapter extend the descriptions here.)

Developmentally Appropriate Practice

The National Association for the Education of Young Children advocates the use of developmentally appropriate practice (DAP), or those practices and materials that make good developmental sense for young children. Jan Duckart, a kindergarten teacher, defines DAP as "what it is reasonable to expect children to do." I've always liked this definition. Jan's interpretation reminds us that DAP involves a careful matching and tailoring of our instructional goals, strategies, and materials to the individual needs and talents of our children. We must know our children, and understand and see critical intersections between children's chronological age, developmental capabilities, cultural and linguistic talents, out-of-school experiences, and history of playing and working with us.

Culturally Responsive Teaching

The attention given in the 1997 DAP position statement to the social and cultural contexts of children provides a link to the concept of culturally responsive teaching (CRT). This concept refers to an educational vision and a collection of teaching strategies that are responsive to children's linguistic and cultural talents and resources. This vision focuses on increasing student achievement and providing high-quality education to students from historically underachieving cultural and linguistic groups. The concept encompasses the physical classroom environment, interpersonal and social interaction in the classroom, curriculum content, language and cultural variety, assessment and testing. CRT validates students in terms of their cultural and linguistic backgrounds, celebrates their talents and resources, and makes room for children's home and community experiences and views of the world.

CRT also emphasizes the value of group collaboration and social inclusion in the intellectual life of the classroom. Alonzo Williams, a kindergarten teacher, likes to do whole-group interactive writing whereby each child's contribution is for the whole class. So when children write and contribute to a class text, they are writing not just for themselves but for everyone—"I like to make this activity as inclusive as possible and to give the children a lot of power to write. I'm putting the pen in their hands for all of us."

Montessori Approach

Maria Montessori advocated the value of children's senses—sight, smell, touch, thought, emotion—as integrally involved in language and literacy learning. In this education of the senses, young children are afforded rich daily opportunities with which to explore and experience the sights and sounds of letters, words, and language. For example, Montessori programs employ well-made sensory materials that allow children to explore the different shapes that the letters of the alphabet make through sandpaper letters and individual letters made out of other materials with various surfaces. In children's first experiences in writing the letters of the alphabet, they further experience the letter shapes through writing in loose sand and salt as additional sensory experiences in written language. In all of these and other experiences with letters and words, the overall goal is for literacy learning to be based on children's tactile experiences with the concrete letters and objects. The more abstract challenge of visually discriminating and writing the letters only from sight is a later step in the process of sense exploration and development.

Project Approach

The project approach is based upon children's own emerging interests in themselves, one another, and their immediate worlds. In this approach, teachers do not plan and carry out a yearlong curriculum from a published curriculum series, but rather envision and enact a curriculum according to projects based on children's in-the-moment experiences, questions, ideas, and interests. In this way, the language of children's experiences and their questions—whether about birds or the local fire station or post office or the moon—are the foundation for generating curriculum and activities. Projects can also have certain distinct stages (finding a focus, beginning a project, investigating the topic, and concluding).

In the project approach, children's language and literacy are closely and intimately tied to their developmental understanding of the particular content, experiences, and ideas associated with the projects. For example, a project about the post office may begin after one child has an idea for mailing a letter to her grandmother to invite her to visit the class. The resulting activities can include the teacher guiding and recording a discussion of the children's past experiences with visiting the post office, brainstorming what the children think they will see on a future trip to the post office, visiting the post office and drawing and dictating about it, and then revisiting the initial list to compare the children's initial knowledge of post offices.

Reggio Emilia Approach

An innovative early childhood model from Italy, the Reggio Emilia approach emphasizes curriculum grounded in children's own interests and projects carried out over several weeks and even months. Reggio Emilia values group discussion and social collaboration in furthering children's understanding of their emerging physical, artistic, social, cultural, and scientific worlds. The primary process for this exploration is through art and language, and children are provided with artistic tools and resources for exploring their ideas and theories.

Projects begin with the children's interests and curiosities. For instance, children and teachers may take up a project on shadows as sparked by the interest of a few children in the effects of the sun's changing position in the sky. The teachers and children then embark on a journey that does not follow a prescribed or preset curriculum for using art and other symbolic means such as writing to understand the nature of shadows. The steps in this journey are often initiated by the children, from whom the teachers take cues in providing new materials and new strategies for promoting the children's understanding. The teachers, children, and their families engage in a process of documentation, in which particular aspects of the process are recorded and represented through drawings, writings, and photographs. This documentation records particular findings on the part of the children and shows the chronological and developmental journeys that the children undertook as they discussed, drew, enacted, and thought about shadows. The documentation material is then assembled in a formal way into a series of panels that are publicly displayed and shared within the school community.

APPROACHES TO EARLY LITERACY TEACHING AND LEARNING

We have a wealth of ideas, models, and programs for creating and implementing powerful and rich literacy teaching. In this section, I describe ideas associated with selected approaches for early literacy teaching and learning. In actual teaching practice, the particular mix and combination of elements from these approaches is up to us—we as teachers envision our literacy education, implement our curriculum drawing on a number of approaches, observe children's learning, and adjust our teaching.

Reading Readiness

Reading readiness refers to the idea that children are "ready" to learn to read and write because their cognitive, linguistic, and social capabilities have developed to a level at which they can attend to and process the oral and visual cues and components involved in reading and writing. This idea of readiness has become popular once again as selected language arts programs and models of literacy teaching emphasize the steady progression of skills and abilities that children need for successful literacy acquisition.

There are several components and factors cited as most critical for reading readiness (see Figure 2.1). There are other factors considered helpful in promoting reading readiness. These include the ability to sit still for long periods (for focused reading instruction), knowledge of story language ("Once upon a time") and of story structure (a beginning, middle, and end), ability to use specialized reading terms (*long vowel*, *short vowel*, *silent* e), and the ability to read Standard English texts.

Basal Reading Series

The reading readiness framework has been most closely aligned with the use of published reading series or what are sometimes referred

Figure 2.1. Components of Reading Readiness

Component	Definition	Example
Phonemic Awareness	Knowledge of linguistic sounds and ability to auditorally discriminate between sounds as represented by individual and groups of letters	Hearing and recognizing the difference between the sounds /b/ and /p/ in the words *bat* and *pat*; distinguishing between the sounds /s/ and /sh/ in *sag* and *shag*
Phonics	Instruction in building on children's phonemic awareness and knowledge of sound-symbol relationships; matching sounds and letters to read or decode text (the term *phonetics* refers to the range of possible sounds in languages and is not a term used in teaching and education)	Using the knowledge of the sounds (/b/, /a/, /t/) that *b* and *a* and *t* make and putting them together or blending them into /bat/ for *bat*
Segmentation and Blending	Pulling apart and putting together combinations of sounds and letters	Segmentation: *bat* when pulled apart is composed of the individual sounds /b/, /a/, and /t/ Blending: *bat* is put together by blending together the letters *b* and *a* and *t*
Letter Identification	Knowledge of the letter "names" of the 26 letters in the English alphabet or corresponding symbols in another language; in any language these letter names are arbitrary and mostly learned from rote memory	*a* and *z* have the different letter names that sound like /ay/ and /zee/
Letter Sound Identification	Knowledge of the sounds that each letter of the alphabet makes	The letter *a* can sound like /a/ in *cat*, like /a/ in *David* and *make*, like /a/ in *am* and *any*, like /a/ in *ability*
Visual Discrimination	Ability to discriminate between letter shapes and words	Distinguishing between similarly shaped letters such as *b* and *d* as well as between letters such as *f* and *z*, which look more dissimilar
Print Awareness	Knowledge that printed text has meaning and a message	Asking an adult to read a book and asking an adult to read "what it says"
Book Knowledge	Knowledge of the front of a book, left-to-right text orientation, and page-turning	Holding a book by first looking at the cover right-side-up, then turning the book page by page from the left to the right

to as basal reading textbooks. Basal readers are often organized according to reading levels—from easiest to most difficult—for children's ease of learning and teachers' ease of teaching and instruction. In other words, the readability levels of the texts increase as children improve their decoding and reading skills. The reading texts are often organized around a scope or set of reading skills and knowledge that are laid out according to a predetermined sequence or order of presentation and instruction. In this model, children at the kindergarten level first learn such basic literacy skills as letter and sound identification, and then move on to simple sight words and phonics activities. The overall goal, like the idea of reading readiness, is to build a foundation of reading skills that allows young children to become more independent, accurate, and fluent readers as they progress through a reading series. Published reading series are currently quite popular because they are aligned at the primary-grade level with state language arts standards and frameworks. They are useful for teachers, especially new teachers, because they provide a collection of materials (big books, small books, multiple copies, multilingual books, teacher's guide, audiotapes, workbooks, homework folders, family support materials, overheads) that are readily accessible and convenient to use.

Emergent Literacy

The idea of emergent literacy arose over the past 20 years partly in reaction to and against the reading readiness model. The approach, which has been associated with the whole language movement of the 1980s, emphasizes children's natural discovery of the forms and functions of written language. In an emergent literacy approach, children do not learn to read and write based on a step-by-step model of learning a prescribed set of basic literacy skills. In this view, children are *already* reading and writing, though they are most likely not doing so in a conventional sense of decoding text or writing whole words. A 4-year-old who memorizes stories and writes in scribbles is reading and writing because he or she is engaged with printed and written symbols.

According to emergent literacy, children learn literacy as they come to it rather than as it comes to them, and children engage themselves and one another in meaningful and motivating experiences with sounds, letters, words, texts, and stories. Literacy instruction is therefore not contingent on a set or list of attributes or elements that children need to have in place before they are ready to learn to read and write. Children's engagement with books, reading, and writing is more holistic and well-rounded, as reading and writing activities are based upon children's natural sense of curiosity and discovery and integrated into a classroom's overall curriculum and content.

Language Experience Approach

In the language experience approach, children dictate a text or a story or a label for a drawing, and an adult or older child writes it down in the child's language. This approach uses children's oral language talents and resources as a personal and social link to literacy. Starting with children's oral language, which is more sophisticated and complex in structure and content than their written-language knowledge, we can extend and transfer it to writing. This process of oral to written language is immediate and children can instantly see and hear the transformation of their spoken words on the written page. It is an effective teaching strategy for all children, and it greatly benefits English-language learners, who can begin their literacy learning on the basis of their oral language knowledge of the second language.

The approach can be used with whole-class, small-group, partner, and individual learning formats and groupings. In our teaching small and large groups of children, language experience activities help us write down children's ideas and then revisit them later for further exploration and discussion. In Alonzo's kindergarten class, the children dictated a text based on a recent field trip:

> We went to Hidden Villa Farm. We got on a big bus with
> t.v.'s. We drove on the freeway and counted the red cars and
> green signs. Then we ate snacks and looked at the animals.
> Then we went to go get some pumpkins. Then we ate lunch
> and played. We got back on the bus to go to school. The field
> trip was fun. The End.

Alonzo displays this and other language experience products around his classroom so that "children can access the information."

Children's Literature—Multicultural and Multilingual

Children's literature can be used both for literacy involvement (participating in book experiences, story discussions, and reading for enjoyment) and also for literacy instruction (learning from teachers that increases children's literacy knowledge and orchestration of literacy skills). In both instances, children need daily access to high-quality, multicultural, and multilingual books of varied sizes, content, and linguistic and literary forms. Further, the opportunity to hold, listen to, and read outstanding children's literature provides a critical developmental connection back to children's book explorations (chewing on books, looking at pictures, listening to the sounds and rhythm of books) when they were infants and toddlers.

Providing interaction with high-quality children's literature books on a daily basis fosters a lifelong memory and love for reading. A memory for books comes not so much from simply starting with books early as it does from engaging in literature with interested peers and adults early on. Children's literature that features content, language, and images that accurately and powerfully portray children from varied cultural and linguistic traditions engages children in the power of the spoken and written word. These books can come in a variety of forms and genres: stories, fairy tales, riddles and jokes, folktales and myths, historical fiction, poetry, content or informational books, and concept books. Children can interact with children's literature at a variety of levels. Through daily read-alouds, such literature allows children to comprehend content and stories without the added challenge of actually reading and decoding the texts on their own. Similarly, for English-language learners, read-alouds encourage listening for the unfamiliar sounds, constructions, and word meanings of a new language without the children having to attend to the reading tasks of decoding and comprehension.

Writing Process Approach

In the 1970s, teachers and researchers primarily from the United States, Great Britain, Australia, and New Zealand took a great interest in improving the teaching of writing to young children. These writing proponents argued that we need to pay more attention to the forms and functions of children's writing, and that strengthening children's writing would also improve their reading. The writing process approach is based on the model of adult professional writers who create writing topics and then engage in a long process of revising and redrafting their work for a particular audience. The form of the writing process approach that is advocated for children involves these components: children choose their own writing topics, talk and interact with peers as they write, conference with peers and teachers about their writing, undertake a series of redrafts of the original written piece, write a final published piece, share this piece with an audience, and place their best work in their writing portfolio.

Throughout the writing process, teachers take on the role of coach and facilitator, teaching mini-lessons on selected aspects of writing form and function and provide one-to-one support and guidance for children throughout the process. For spelling, children are encouraged to spell as best they can, listening to the discrete sounds of the words and matching them to corresponding letters and letter combinations. This strategy was originally referred to as invented spelling, and is now more commonly known as developmental and best-guess spelling. Alonzo Williams, the kindergarten teacher, refers to children's early spelling as phonemic writing, and stresses the importance of children "not getting stuck on correct spelling" at the expense of seeing themselves as interested, motivated writers.

Over many years of teaching, I have blended and combined elements of all of these approaches to early literacy teaching and learning. I have taken the conceptual ideas and practical strategies that I like and created my own personal philosophy and vision for children's early literacy education. We must remember that this is a long-term process—of understanding the approaches, experimenting with the ideas and strategies in actual practice, and reflecting upon their value for our particular teaching settings, our children, and our families. To avoid the frequent pendulum swings in early literacy from one approach to another, we need to avoid looking for short-term solutions. Rather, we need to take our time, getting to know a range of approaches through our own crafting and learning, shaping others' ideas to make good teaching sense for us and our children.

LITERACY EVALUATION AND ASSESSMENT

Literacy evaluation refers to determining what we initially need to teach and how; it also indicates understanding the effectiveness of our teaching and the children's learning. Evaluation is the process of determining, in the course of ongoing observation and understanding of our teaching and the children's learning, the directions and tools and materials for literacy teaching. Assessment, then, follows evaluation and helps tell us what is working well and possible new directions to take to strengthen our teaching. Assessment informs the teaching-learning relationship and provides us with information, insights, and ideas for understanding and seeing new ways to improve teaching.

In current literacy education, standards and testing tell us what to teach and often how to do it; this takes away our impetus to make our own informed decisions on the direction of our literacy teaching. We are left, then, only with the task of assessment *after* teaching—and then primarily with the goal of assessing what the standards are dictating be taught and learned. This shortsighted view of evaluation and assessment does not deepen our understanding of the teaching-learning relationship in literacy education. Moreover, it makes for a short memory, on our part, of what we need to teach and what the children need to learn—we need to teach letter identification because we need to assess the children's letter knowledge three times a year in kindergarten. This only provides us with information on what a child does or does not know, and not how we can improve our teaching and our children's learning in sophisticated ways.

Concepts About Print

Concepts about print refers to children's emerging understanding of the forms and functions of print and written language. Specifically, concepts of print include such literacy features as children's knowledge that print has meaning and a message, that books in English are opened and turned a certain way, that we read from top to bottom and from left to right on a printed page, and that we understand basic punctuation (a capital letter to begin sentence, a period to end sentence). We can understand this in a formal way through a concepts about print assessment (see Marie Clay's materials). This form of assessment yields valuable basic information on children's book and print knowledge. The assessment measure does not take a long time to carry out and provides detailed data that is easily translated into literacy instruction and curriculum.

We can complement formal assessment through informal data collection of children's understanding of concepts of print as they work and play. For instance, teachers can observe and document children's awareness of print by noting when and where children copy print, use words displayed around the classroom for their writing and spelling, and read and use words from children's literature and nonfiction sources in classroom libraries. Some children will exhibit their understanding of books and print more accurately in informal situations—when book browsing and reading with friends—than in the more formal setting of a concepts of print assessment measure. They feel more comfortable interacting with print in a natural way than during a formal assessment.

Running Records

Running records are a straightforward assessment measure that do not require a lot of material and can be used with books used within the kindergarten classroom for regular reading development. Running records yield both qualitative and quantitative data and encourage teachers to closely observe the reading behaviors and performance of individual children. In a running record, teachers or other adults focus on understanding the strengths and weaknesses of children's oral reading or oral decoding of selected texts. Children begin with the easiest-to-read texts and then move up to more and more difficult texts as they gain accuracy, fluency, intonation, and expression. Controlled vocabulary is used to have each text at a different reading level or level of readability. In a typical running record, an adult asks the child to read out-loud a selected text or passage and as the child reads, the adult marks selected aspects of the child's reading successes, strategies, and errors. For instance, data are recorded on the child's use of the pictures to help in reading the text, level of success with sound-symbol correspondence, possible reversal or transposition of sounds within a single word, awareness of basic punctuation, reading intonation and expression as indicative of understanding the text, the number and kind of attempts to reread or self-correct certain words or syllables, and sound-symbol or whole-word miscues that interfere with reading comprehension and those that don't impede the child's understanding of the phrase or sentence.

Child Observation and Teacher Research

There is a long tradition in early childhood education of the close observation and documentation of children's language and literacy learning. This emphasis has received a recent boost with the work by Reggio

Emilia educators and others devoted to the documentation of children's learning. Teachers observe children's development, growth, thinking, and learning as children interact with materials, ideas, resources, peers, teachers, and families. This makes for a rich and sophisticated foundation for our attempts to understand children's learning.

Other forms of child observation and documentation can also be carried out through various forms of teacher research. Teacher research, sometimes referred to as practitioner inquiry and action research, involves teachers and other practitioners researching their own teaching and learning contexts. For example, the keeping of teaching journals and diaries of selected literacy activities, strategies, and issues provide daily information and reflections on how well our teaching is going and how well the children are responding. In this process, teacher researchers use tape recorders, video recorders, conventional cameras, and digital cameras for capturing children's talk and behaviors. Other forms of teacher research can focus on particular areas of the classroom, such as the writing center or the classroom library, and teacher researchers can spend weeks and months observing and recording children's interactions with literacy and the development and growth of certain literacy forms and functions in these particular areas. Teacher researchers also may enlist the research help of their students, as teachers and children collaborate on gathering data and analyzing the information connected with a particular literacy project or activity. This kind of teacher research project allows teachers to have an additional window into the thoughts and ideas of children and to understand their thinking and feelings through the children's own words and writings.

Child observation and teacher research can yield detailed data on children's learning and teacher effectiveness. They provide teachers with direct evidence of the success of a particular strategy or the worthiness of a particular activity or project. These tools can also help teachers understand underlying processes and factors that may be hindering children from working or playing at their potential abilities. Some of these assessment and observation approaches can be time-consuming and often need to be carried out on an almost daily basis. It is helpful for teacher researchers and others employing these strategies to collaborate with colleagues in analyzing journal notes, classroom observations, and samples of student work and play.

Tracking Language and Literacy Growth

Given the rapid and dramatic language and literacy changes that young children experience during the preschool and kindergarten years, it is a conceptual and procedural challenge to understand children's ever-changing literacy learning. For instance, during the preschool years, this can mean differences in expectation and curriculum for 3-year-olds versus for 4- and 5-year-olds. The two forms of the Language and Literacy Developmental Profile (LLDP; see Appendix A) is one way to track children's language and literacy growth during the preschool years, and it can be adapted for kindergartners. Based on input from both preschool and kindergarten teachers, I designed the two forms to be age and literacy knowledge specific regarding where children might be developmentally. There is also important crossover of literacy components between the two forms for the two age groups (such as the emphasis on playing with language and listening to read-alouds), and this shows the importance of connecting our teaching across 3- to 5-year-old developmental span. The LLDP also contains components for supporting English-language learners and bilingual learners and for tracking vocabulary growth, syntactical understanding, and biliteracy.

The Preschool to Kindergarten Information Sheet (PKIS; see Appendix B), to be filled out by preschool teachers, is designed for children's kindergarten teachers. As such, it is an informational sheet for strengthening the preschool-to-kindergarten transition. The LLDP is to be included with this form for the kindergarten teacher. Both the LLDP and PKIS are to be sent early to the kindergarten teachers before the start of the school year so that preschool and kindergarten teachers have time to confer regarding each child's language, literacy, and general development. In this way, the LLDP and the PKIS are a built-in structure for yearly communication between preschool and kindergarten teachers, and as the forms are revised from time to time, this further encourages the teachers to dialogue and collaborate on the critical preschool-to-kindergarten transition.

Portfolio Assessment

Portfolios are often called forms of alternative or authentic assessment. In portfolio assessment, children and adults systematically collect and store children's work over the course of a year or more. In some preschools and elementary schools, children's portfolios continue on with the child as they move to the following level, whether within a school or on to the following grade, and children's future teachers continue adding selected pieces of the children's work and play. When children are asked to contribute to portfolio assessment, they are asked to assess and choose their best pieces of work or those products that they are most proud of. These are then dated and placed in chronological order within the portfolios. Children can also contribute their own comments on their work—"This is my best piece of writing because I learned to spell some new words" or "I am really proud of this poem because I wrote it in both English and Spanish"—and serve as co-assessors of their own ongoing progress and development. At the end of the school year, children can be invited to prepare an overall assessment of and reflection on their entire portfolio—"I'm most proud of the artwork that I did this year in preschool" or "I'm most proud of the stories that I wrote this year about my grandma and my grandpa"—and the portfolios are sent home. To save space, portfolios or selections of material can be scanned into a computer for e-mailing to families or to be put onto a compact disk. Families can also become involved in portfolio assessment as they are encouraged to select pieces of student work that they feel are representative of their children's best or most accomplished work and play.

Fostering a memory for literacy takes in our conceptual understanding of children's literacy development, our philosophies and visions for literacy education, our tools and strategies for teaching, and our methods of evaluating and assessing the effectiveness of our teaching. Powerful literacy teaching is based upon a conviction that we are the primary movers of children's literacy learning and that we are the ones guiding what we teach, how we teach, and how we understand our teaching. We must begin with the conviction that we teach for our literacy memories—those of our children and our own—and that memories are made and created in the moment and at the beginning. Literacy memories do not come about later on, in May or June of a preschool or kindergarten year. Rather, a rich and uplifting literacy "program" begins *before* children enter our classrooms, as memories for literacy are embedded within a deep understanding of how and why our children might best learn and grow as readers and writers.

Suggested Activities

1. Think back to your early school days. Make a list of your early literacy experiences and then match them to the ideas and strategies presented in this chapter. Which ideas and strategies are most prominent? Consider how you might incorporate a few into your teaching.
2. If you work with African American children, make a list of their language and literacy talents and resources. Make another list of your instructional strategies and activities that incorporate and reflect the children's language and literacy talents and resources. How might you integrate even more of the children's knowledge and experiences into your literacy teaching?
3. If you work with English-language learners, make a web of their literacy needs. Make another web depicting the strategies that the English-language learners use. Connect a need with a strategy and consider how you can strengthen this connection in your teaching.
4. Choose a few families with whom you work or families whom you know from outside school. In one column, generate several questions that they might have regarding literacy education for their children. In the next column, formulate possible answers for each one of the questions that you could communicate to the families. In a third column, write responses that the families might make in regard to your answers.

USEFUL RESOURCES

Language Variety, Literacy, and Culture

Baugh, J. (1999). *Out of the mouths of slaves: African American language and educational malpractice*. Austin: University of Texas Press.

Delpit, L. (1995). *Other people's children: Cultural conflict in the classroom*. New York: Free Press.

Heath, S. B. (1982). What no bedtime story means: Narrative skills at home and school. *Language in Society, 11*(2), 49–76.

Labov, W. (1977). *Language in the inner city: Studies in the Black English vernacular*. Philadelphia: University of Pennsylvania Press.

Rickford, J. (1999). *African American vernacular English*. Oxford: Basil Blackwell.

Smitherman, G. (1977). *Talkin and testifyin: The language of Black America*. Boston: Houghton Mifflin.

Biliteracy

Ballenger, C. (1999). *Teaching other people's children: Literacy and learning in a bilingual classroom*. New York: Teachers College Press.

Gregory, E. (1996). *Making sense of a new world: Learning to read in a second language*. London: Paul Chapman.

Reyes, M. de la luz, & Halcon, J. (Eds.). (2001). *The best for our children: Critical perspectives on literacy for Latino children*. New York: Teachers College Press.

Valdés, G. (2001). *Learning and not learning English: Latino students in American schools*. New York: Teachers College Press.

Wang, J., Inhoff A., & Chen, H.-C. (1999). *Reading in Chinese script: A cognitive analysis*. Mahwah, NJ: Erlbaum.

Developmentally Appropriate Practice

Bredekamp, S., & Copple, C. (Eds.). (1997). *Developmentally appropriate practice in early childhood programs* (Rev. ed.). Washington, DC: National Association for the Education of Young Children.

Bredekamp, S., Copple, C., & Neuman, S. B. (2000). *Learning to read and write: Developmentally appropriate practices for young children*. Washington, DC: National Association for the Education of Young Children.

Bredekamp, S., & Neuman, S. B. (2000). Becoming a reader: A developmentally appropriate approach. In D. S. Strickland & L. M. Morrow (Eds.), *Beginning reading and writing* (pp. 22–35). New York: Teachers College Press.

Jipson, J. (1991). Developmentally appropriate practice: Culture, curriculum, connections. *Early Education and Development, 2*(2), 120–136.

Mallory, B. L., & New, R. S. (Eds.). (1994). *Diversity and developmentally appropriate practices: Challenges for early childhood education*. New York: Teachers College Press.

Meier, D. R. (2000). *Scribble scrabble: Learning to read and write with diverse children, teachers, and families*. New York: Teachers College Press.

Schickendanz, J. A. (1999). *Much more than the ABCs: The early stages of reading and writing*. Washington, DC: National Association for the Education of Young Children.

Montessori Approach

Montessori, M. (1964). *The Montessori method*. New York: Shocken Books.
Montessori, M. (1967). *The absorbent mind*. New York: Henry Holt.

Project Approach

Gardner, H., Feldman, D. H., & Krechevsky, M. (1998). *Building on children's strengths: The exploration of project spectrum* (Vol. 1). New York: Teachers College Press. *http://ericee.org/project.html*
Helm, J. H., & Beneke, S. (Eds.). (2003). *The power of projects: Meeting contemporary challenges in early childhood classrooms*. New York: Teachers College Press.
Katz, L., & Chard, S. (1989). *Engaging children's minds: The project approach*. Greenwich, CT: Ablex.
LeeKeenan, D., & Edwards, C. P. (1992). Using the project approach with toddlers. *Young Children, 47*(4), 31–36.

Reggio Emilia Approach

Cadwell, L. B. (2003). *Bringing learning to life: The Reggio approach to early childhood education*. New York: Teachers College Press.
Edwards, C., Gandini, L., & Forman, G. (Eds.). (1998). *The hundred languages of children: The Reggio Emilia approach to early childhood education* (2nd ed.). Norwood, NJ: Ablex.
Giudici, C., Rinaldi, C., & Krechevsky, M. (Eds.). (2001). *Making learning visible: Children as individual and group learners*. Reggio Emilia, Italy: Reggio Children. Distributed through the National Association for the Education of Young Children.
Kennedy, D. K. (1996). After Reggio Emilia: May the conversation begin. *Young Children, 51*(5), 24–27.
Stremmel, A. J., Fu, V. R., & Hill, L. T. (Eds.). (2002). *Teaching and learning: Collaborative exploration of the Reggio Emilia approach*. Upper Saddle River, NJ: Merrill/Prentice Hall.

Culturally Responsive Teaching

Bowman, B. (Ed.). (2003). *Love to read: Essays on developing and enhancing early literacy skills of African American children*. Washington, DC: National Association for the Education of Young Children.
García, E. (1994). *Understanding and meeting the challenge of student cultural diversity*. Boston, MA: Houghton Mifflin.
Igoa, C. (1995). *The inner world of the immigrant child*. Mahwah, NJ: Lawrence Erlbaum.

Ladson-Billings, G. (1994). *The dreamkeepers: Successful teachers of African American children*. San Francisco, CA: Jossey-Bass.

Lee, C. D. (1994). African-centered pedagogy: Complexities and possibilities. In M. J. Shujaa (Ed.), *Too much schooling, too little education: A paradox of Black life in White societies* (pp. 295–318). Trenton, NJ: Africa World Press.

Nieto, S. (2002). *Language, culture, and teaching: Critical perspectives for a new century*. Mahwah, NJ: Lawrence Erlbaum.

Vasquez, V. M. (2003). *Negotiating critical literacies with young children*. Mahwah, NJ: Lawrence Erlbaum.

Evaluation and Assessment

Bredekamp, S., & Rosegrant, T. (Eds.). (1995). *Reaching potentials: Transforming early childhood curriculum and assessment* (Vol. 2). Washington, DC: National Association for the Education of Young Children.

California Department of Education. (1998). *Assessing the development of a first and a second language in early childhood*. Sacramento: California Department of Education.

Clay, M. (1985). *The early detection of reading difficulties* (3rd ed.). Auckland, NZ: Heinemann.

Clay, M. (1993). *An observation survey of early literacy achievement*. Portsmouth, NH: Heinemann.

Clay, M. (2000). *Running records for classroom teachers*. Auckland, NZ: Heinemann.

Clay, M. (2000). *Concepts about print for teachers of young children*. Auckland, NZ: Heinemann.

Drummond, M. J. (1994). *Learning to see: Assessment through observation*. York, ME: Stenhouse.

Fountas, I. C., & Pinnell, G. S. (1996). *Guided reading: Good first teaching for all children*. Portsmouth, NH: Heinemann.

Gardner, H., Feldman, D. H., & Krechevsky, M. (1998). *Project Zero frameworks: Preschool assessment handbook* (Vol. 3). New York: Teachers College Press.

Genishi, C., & Dyson, A. H. (1984). *Language assessment in the early years*. Cambridge, MA: Harvard University Press.

Gullo, D. (1993). *Understanding assessment and evaluation in early childhood education*. New York: Teachers College Press.

Harp, B., & Brewer, J. A. (2000). Assessing reading and writing in the early years. In D. S. Strickland & L. M. Morrow (Eds.), *Beginning reading and writing* (pp. 154–167). New York: Teachers College Press.

Johnston, P. H. (2000). *Running records: A self-tutoring guide*. York, ME: Stenhouse.

Morrow, L. M., & Smith, J. K. (Eds.). (1990). *Assessment for instruction in early literacy*. Englewood Cliffs, NJ: Prentice Hall.

Roskos, K., & Neumann, S. B. (1994). Of scribbles, schemas, and storybooks: Using literacy albums to document young children's growth. *Young Children, 49*(2), 83.

Yopp, H. K. (1995). A test for assessing phonemic awareness in young children. *The Reading Teacher, 1*(49), 20–29.

Child Observation and Teacher Research

Burnaford, G., Fischer, J., & Hobson, D. (Eds.). (2001). *Teachers doing research: The power of action through inquiry.* Mahwah, NJ: Lawrence Erlbaum Associates.

Cochran-Smith, M., & Lytle, S. (1993). *Inside/outside: Teacher research and knowledge.* New York: Teachers College Press.

Cohen, D. H., Stern, V., & Balaban, N. (1997). *Observing and recording the behavior of young children* (4th ed.). New York: Teachers College Press.

Espiritu, E., Meier, D. R., Villazana-Price, N., & Wong, M. (2002). Promoting teacher research in early childhood: A collaborative project on children's language and literacy learning. *Young Children, 5*(57), 71–79.

Freeman, D. (1998). *Doing teacher research: From inquiry to understanding.* New York: Heinle & Heinle.

Helm, J. H., Beneke, S., & Steinheimer, K. (1998). *Windows on learning: Documenting young children's work.* New York: Teachers College Press.

Himley, M., & Carini, P. F. (Eds.). (2000). *From another angle: Children's strengths and school standards, the Prospect Center's descriptive review of the child.* New York: Teachers College Press.

Hubbard, R. S., & Power, B. M. (1999). *Living the questions: A guide for teacher-researchers.* York, ME: Stenhouse.

Meier, D. R. (1997). *Learning in small moments: Life in an urban classroom.* New York: Teachers College Press.

Stremmel, A. (2002). Nurturing professional and personal growth through inquiry. *Young Children 5*(57), 62–70.

Language Experience Approach

Stauffer, R. G. (1970). *The language-experience approach to the teaching of reading.* New York: Harper & Row.

Stauffer, R. G. (1980). *The language-experience approach to the teaching of reading* (2nd ed.). New York: Harper & Row.

Language, Literacy, and Families

Ada, A. F. (1988). The Pajaro Valley experience: Working with Spanish-speaking parents to develop children's reading and writing skills in the home through the use of children's literature. In T. Skutnabb-Kangas & J. Cummins (Eds.). *Minority education: From shame to struggle* (pp. 223–238). Philadelphia: Multi-Lingual Matters.

Compton-Lilly, C. (2003). *Reading families: The literate lives of urban children.* New York: Teachers College Press.

Delgado-Gaitan, C. (1990). *Literacy for empowerment: The role of parents in children's education.* New York: Falmer Press.

Dickinson, D. K., & Tabors, P. O. (2002). Fostering language and literacy in classrooms and homes. *Young Children, 57*(2), 10–19.

Ditzel, R. J. (2000). *Great beginnings: Creating a literacy-rich kindergarten.* York, ME: Stenhouse.

Gadsden, V. G. (1994). Understanding family literacy: Conceptual issues facing the field. *Teachers College Record*, *96*(1), 78–89.

Gregory, E. (2001). Sisters and brothers as language and literacy teachers: Synergy between siblings playing and working together. *Journal of Early Childhood Literacy*, *1*(3), 301–322.

Gregory, E., Long, S., & Volk, D. (Eds.). (2004). *Many pathways to literacy: Learning with siblings, grandparents, peers, and communities*. London: Routledge.

McCaleb, S. P. (1995). *Building communities of learners: A collaboration among teachers, students, families, and community*. Mahwah, NJ: Lawrence Erlbaum.

Ortiz, R., Stile, S., & Brown, C. (1999). Early literacy activities of fathers: Reading and writing with young children. *Young Children*, *54*(5), 16–18.

Taylor, D., & Dorsey-Gaines, C. (1988). *Growing up literate: Learning from inner-city families*. Portsmouth, NH: Heinemann.

Valdés, G. (1996). *Con respeto: Bridging the distances between culturally diverse families and schools*. New York: Teachers College Press.

Children's Books Cited in Chapter 2

Martin, B., & Carle, E. (1967). *Brown bear, brown bear, What do you see?* New York: Holt, Rinehart and Winston.

Sendak, M. (1963). *Where the wild things are*. New York: Harper & Row.

Strickland, P., & Strickland, H. (1994). *Dinosaur roar!* New York: Dutton.

Chapter 3

Creating a Literacy Environment

DALISHA: I know this one. The letters fall from the tree (preschooler
looking at *Chicka Chicka Boom Boom*).

TEACHING AND LEARNING QUESTIONS

1. Why is the physical environment of the classroom important for literacy learning?
2. What are essential elements for creating an inviting and supportive literacy environment?
3. How can the classroom environment support the literacy learning of English-language and bilingual learners?
4. What are important books to select and why?
5. How can we find new ways to improve our literacy environments?

KEY ELEMENTS OF A LITERACY ENVIRONMENT

Young children associate memories for literacy with the places and settings of their childhoods. There are several key ingredients for establishing a rich and vibrant literacy environment for preschoolers and kindergartners.

Make It Your Own

Our classrooms need to reflect the personal literacy interests and talents that we have as teachers, individuals, writers, and readers. Just as we personalize where we live, we can personalize where we work. So in personalizing our classrooms, we create a place that reflects our personal, cultural, and linguistic backgrounds and interests, and that entices children to enter and stay in the world of school literacy. We can accomplish this by displaying some of our favorite books from our childhoods and early school days, posters of our favorite authors and books, and children's books that we currently read and enjoy. These are also ways for children to see us as models for becoming lifelong readers and writers, for connecting childhood literacy with the literacy of adulthood. Young children need to see and hear adults who are still interested in reading and writing, and children will identify with books and other literacy materials because of their personal connections with us. Personalizing the environment for literacy also sends a message to families—here are some ways to personalize a lit-

eracy environment and make it an attractive and interesting place in which
to talk, read, and write.

Make It Developmentally Appropriate

A developmentally appropriate literacy environment promotes a love
of literature and an active engagement with handling, touching, listening
to, memorizing (committing the text to memory), pretend reading (making up a story line), and looking at books and other reading materials. The
classroom environment needs to match children's developmental capabilities, interests, and dispositions. Chairs, tables, rugs, materials, and resources
need to be within easy reach for all children. I have seen books put up high
on shelves so children can't get to them—but when books and other literacy
materials are visually and physically accessible to children, they feel that
the materials are there for them to use and enjoy. When children enter a
classroom in September and see a rich and vivid display of literacy materials, they get the message that these books are theirs to explore and use over
the year. Children learn by seeing, touching, smelling, listening, tasting. The
children's book author Maurice Sendak has fond memories of early experiences with books—not so much reading them, but chewing, trying to eat,
and smelling them.

When children are afforded comfortable and inviting spaces in the
classroom for reading and writing, and for using and consulting books and
other literacy materials, then they tend to associate the comfort of book
reading with the comfort of a couch or cozy reading corner. Since children
attend school for many years, their school-based literacy experiences become experiences of place. The Reggio Emilia educators create beautiful and
artistic places where children can learn, including private and public places
for reading, writing, and thinking. Just as many children have regular places
for playing or doing literacy at home, they need access to regular places for
literacy in classrooms.

Integrate Literacy and Play

Figure 3.1 shows a preschool block area that integrates block building, pretend play, and language and literacy. This is an excellent example
of using the environment to integrate literacy into a play area and connect
various curriculum goals (cooperation, play, active motor activity) and
developmental domains (mathematics/spatial learning, language, literacy,
social/collaboration) all in one small physical space. The array of wooden
blocks offers children the daily opportunity to explore dimensions of
space, order, and organization either on their own or with others. These
experiences help children develop their knowledge of mathematics and
physics. The large plastic animals placed on top of the block shelves allow
children to use the animals with the blocks. These experiences encourage

Figure 3.1. Block Area

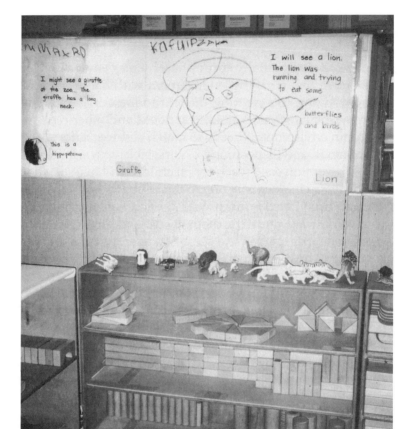

children's pretend play ("let's pretend we're dinosaurs" or "this dinosaur walked on top of your apartment building") and sociodramatic play ("I'm the firefighter and you're the scientist, and we need to find the dinosaurs"), combined with the use of the blocks. The addition of a dry-erase board encourages children (and adults) to draw and write stories about what they built or played with. Without the children being told that they are integrating their learning, the conjunction of the blocks, animals, and dry-erase board offers the children daily opportunities to integrate language, literacy, play, drawing, mathematics, and physics.

Literacy can be integrated into other play areas of the classroom. For instance, in the play house, literacy can be both an ongoing part of this play area and also a temporary special feature. The play house can include everyday household objects (toothpaste boxes, cereal boxes, milk containers) with labels and print in different languages. Children are familiar with these objects, will use them in their dramatic play, and will learn to copy, read, and write the labels over time.

Evaluate and Change the Environment

As teachers, we can always alter what we start. We can always move and change how we have set up an environment for literacy. The effectiveness of the environment can be monitored and followed in a number of ways:

- Recording or taking notes on the involvement of certain children in literacy areas
- Taking photos of children's reading and writing and other literacy behaviors
- Watching for "literacy carry-over" from one designated literacy area to another
- Observing rich and interesting conversations fostered in a literacy area
- Recording language and literacy engagement by English-language and bilingual learners
- Noting children's own suggestions for improving a certain area or space
- Compiling dated selections of the children's literacy products into a portfolio to provide a chronological account of their engagement and learning

We should not set the environment in place in September and think that it needs to stay the same over the course of a school year.

Although too much change in the environment confuses children, it will help strengthen children's literacy learning if the environment is altered as needed. For example, one year I noticed that only a few of my kindergarten children were selecting books from the classroom library. Looking at the bookshelves, I realized that there were simply too many books on the shelves. I reduced the total number of books by one half and turned the books around so the children could see the covers, and the result was dramatic—the majority of the children started to use the library and read the books.

Another year, I realized partway through the year that I had placed the library too far away from the rug area. When I dismissed children from the rug at the end of the day, it was too far for them to walk to select a book to take home with them. I moved the library closer to the rug, which made for a shorter distance for the children to cover, and it was easier for me to monitor the book selection from my position on the rug. The same year, I wanted the children to talk about and interact more with books, so I found a large wooden table and placed it directly in the middle of the classroom. I covered the table with a tablecloth and spread out a rotating display of books for the children to look at and read. It become a new reading area that children could come to and go from as they pleased.

Emphasize Environmental Print

Environmental print refers to printed material displayed in the class-room, which helps children learn to read the names for objects, materials, and places. From a young age, children begin recognizing and trying to "read" print in their home and community environments. (A parent once told me that her 3-year-old daughter thought that the *M* in McDonald's signs stood for *Mother*.) Examples of classroom environmental print in-clude household materials in the playhouse, labels for activity areas and materials, posters, the daily classroom schedule, class job chart, word walls, language experience charts, photographs with text, and children's name cards. Environmental print also needs to be interactive and a daily part of children's literacy work and play. Kaitlin, a kindergarten teacher, has her children—and their parents or siblings who may be bringing them to school—participate in a brief activity upon entering the classroom in the morning. Figure 3.2 shows one kind of chart that Kaitlin uses when children first enter her classroom in the morning. On a large piece of chart paper she has printed the question, "Did you think the turnip would come out?" The children are asked to write their name under "Yes" or "No." This activity is both developmentally and culturally responsive and is an excellent example of making environmental print come alive in an interest-ing and yet simple routine. The simple question was based on a Tolstoy folktale that the class knew well, and so all the children had the back-ground knowledge to answer. The question itself was simply phrased, and it was readable by some of the kindergartners themselves. For the chil-dren who could not read it, the picture of the turnip helped and so did the simple "yes" and "no" responses; or the question could be read by an older sibling or an adult accompanying the child. If a child came into the classroom alone, having arrived by school bus, he or she could easily ask another child for help in reading the question and figuring out what to do. The print here in this example, then, becomes both a part of the physi-cal environment *and*—most important—a part of the social and academic fabric of the classroom.

Figure 3.2. Sign-In Sheet for Children

Environmental print helps support English-language learners and teaches other children vocabulary in other languages. Multilingual labels for classroom objects and areas validate children's first languages and promote second-language acquisition. Figure 3.3 shows activity area and material labels in English, Tagalog, and Spanish. English-language learners will learn to associate a place in the classroom with the corresponding English words (*house, library, art*), and children learning a second language can acquire new vocabulary (*biblioteca, ceramica, ciencia*). Using multilingual labels offers children the advantage of comparing words in different languages. For example, children can see the similarities between the English *art* and the Spanish *arte*, and the Tagalog *relo* and the Spanish *reloj*. (Of course, these languages are given as examples; the particular languages used can vary.) The children themselves can write the labels and draw pictures for illustration. The labels do not have to stay affixed to the materials or activity areas; they can be taken off (Velcro works well), and children can play a game of reaffixing the labels back where they belong.

Allow Permeable Boundaries for Activities

In shaping the physical space of a classroom for literacy, English-language learners and others learning a second language need permeable activity boundaries. This means that children have freedom and a mea-

Figure 3.3. Activity Area and Material Labels in English, Tagalog, and Spanish

English	Tagalog	Spanish
library	aklatan	biblioteca
house	bahay	casa
art	sining	arte
rabbit	koneho	conejo
science	agham	ciencia
frogs	palaka	sapos
listening (area)	pakingan	escuchando
clay	luwad	cerámica
calendar	calendario	calendario
books	aklat	libros
clock	relo	reloj
sand	buhangin	arena
water	tubig	agua
kitchen	lutuan	cocina
writing	sulatan	escribiendo
family information	kaalaman ng maganak	información para padres
teacher's desk	lamesa ng guro	escritorio del maestro
dolls	manika	muñecas
pens and pencils	lapis at bolpen	plumas y lápices
paper	papel	papel
mailboxes	buson	buzon de correo

sure of control for choosing their literacy activities and how and where they work and play. This is most successful when the boundaries or parameters for literacy work and play are somewhat permeable—children are not required to sit still at desks or at one particular activity area for long periods of time. This also means that we as teachers are always on the move and often have to bring the literacy activity *to* children rather than the children coming to us. The early childhood educator Bev Boss advocates a mobile strategy for taking preschool children's dictation, whereby teachers hold clipboards with pens and as they walk around and interact with children, they engage in on-the-spot dictated stories and comments with the children. This means that there is not one specific dictation place or area in the classroom, or one particular dictation time during the day, but that it is a roving activity that children can participate in at any place and at almost any time. This brings greater fluidity and spontaneity to the activity for both children and adults.

In another example of a permeable boundary for literacy work and play, I visited Norma Villazana-Price's preschool and was fascinated to see how a small wooden landing with steps, between the front door and the outside playground, served as an impromptu literacy space. The teachers place a basket of books on the top step for children to browse through and read, and they often sit beside the basket to read with the children. As the children go to and fro between the classrooms and the yard, they stop and participate in the book browsing or the story time. Some children sit down for long periods while others remain standing, leaning over a teacher's shoulder to catch part of a book or story, before continuing on with their other interests in the environment. Both the mobile dictation and the books on the landing are excellent examples of ways to create permeable activity boundaries that make good developmental sense for children and good teaching sense for adults.

Designate Library Areas

Manuel Kichi Wong, a preschool educator, recommends that classroom spaces for literacy encourage intimacy for conversations. Placing the book or library area near the block or art area or near the main doorway of the classroom might result in too much noise and too many interruptions. A reading area need not be complicated, and often the simpler the better— a comfortable rug, a few pillows, and plenty of books within easy reach of children's hands are usually all that is required.

It is most useful to have one central place from which children can choose books and other reading materials, and then other smaller areas to which children can take books and read alone or with a partner. I know a preschool classroom with a reading area consisting of a simple wooden box, a soft pillow, and a tasteful canopy made of fabric, all comfortably nestled into the corner of the classroom. Corners are some of the hardest areas of a room to use well, and the teacher's addition of an attractive canopy overhead makes for a restful spot for children's book reading and conversation.

Feature Certain Books and Literacy Materials

A special area can showcase books and other literacy materials associated with a special area of study or project, focusing on, for example, such content as

- A particular author (Lucille Clifton, Maurice Sendak, Alma Flor Ada, Shel Silverstein, Allen Say)
- A literary genre (fairy tales, alphabet books, folktales, trickster tales, tall tales, legends, rhymes, songs, Mother Goose)
- A theme or topic (friendship, the moon, Día de los Muertos [Day of the Dead], firefighters, architecture)

- Literacy knowledge (rhyming words, homophones and homonyms, antonyms, long vowels, short vowels, letter identification)
- Different languages (numbers, words, greetings, sayings, and phrases in a variety of languages)
- Special books (library books from the school library or from the local public library)
- Project work that has arisen from the children's interests and explorations (things that move, bugs, shadows, the forest, the classroom bird, local nursing home, local homeless shelter)

For example, Kaitlin created a simple display of books on folktales in her kindergarten classroom. She arranged the books—standing up and with the covers opened outward so the children could see—on a table near the classroom meeting area and the classroom's main entrance. The secret to this display, and others like it, is to show only several books, and only those that are actively used by teachers and children. Since in Kaitlin's room, these special display books were placed near the busiest doorway in the classroom, children and parents could easily view them as they entered the room at the beginning and end of the day. For the special books to receive maximum attention from children and families, and to be interwoven into the social and academic life of the classroom, they need to be in a prominent position within the physical space of the classroom.

Provide a Writing and Drawing Center

A writing and drawing center in the classroom signals to children that we take their writing and drawing as seriously as we do their reading development. Many teachers set aside a particular area of the classroom devoted solely to the provision of writing and drawing materials such as the following:

- Pens, markers, crayons, various kinds of paper (lined, unlined, plain, thick and thin, different sizes and textures and colors)
- Letter and shape stencils, scissors, tape, glue, rulers
- Small chalkboards with erasers
- Letter tiles (plastic, wood, painted, outlined in glue/glitter and sand)
- Small trays filled with sand for letter and word writing and outlining
- Staplers, hole punchers, various kinds of bookmaking materials (felt, ribbon, cloth, yarn, string, brads, rubber bands)
- Student-made or teacher-designed word dictionaries or lists of frequently spelled words
- Alphabet strips and characters (Chinese, for example) and words in other languages for children to copy and write

- Photocopied sheets of children's photographs, clipboards, stacks of premade writing/drawing journals
- Envelopes and frames for the children's pictures
- Children's mailboxes for sending and exchanging messages

A typewriter and computers can also be included. I have found, though, that when computers are placed in the writing center, children do not write and draw on paper and are instead attracted to the computer for games. Thus it is often more beneficial to have a separate computer area. I include a typewriter in the writing center because it provides a tactile, and aural, experience that children love. They can type out letters and messages on their own—preschoolers and kindergartners will type random letters and made-up words, their names, names of others, and some words and sentences in correct conventional spelling. The addition of an overhead projector and light table also support children's writing and drawing. By using pens to draw and write on overhead projector sheets, or other kinds of large and small sheets of plastic, children can project their images and words onto a large screen or see them through a light table.

Use Print for Daily Routines

It is beneficial to maximize the print associated with a classroom's daily routines. Examples of such print materials include the daily schedule, monthly calendar, morning message, quote or word of the day, puzzle or math problem of the day or week, star student of the day or week, and special upcoming events. For example, a morning message provides a daily opportunity for whole-class reading, attention to letter and sound identification, word recognition, and community building through discussion of classroom activities and events. The message can be written in languages other than English, and for English-language learners it is helpful to add pictures and drawings to support the written text. I wrote the morning message in my kindergarten classroom *as* the children entered the room in the morning; this enabled the children to see the process of my writing the message (forming the letters, writing from top to bottom and from left to right), and also to participate in an impromptu way (I could ask a child to spell a word or identify a letter for a certain sound). The message can also be composed later with the children as they dictate or write parts of the message with and for one another.

Post Alphabet Charts

Since young children learning to write often forget what the letters of the alphabet look like and need to look directly at the letters as they write, accessible alphabet charts are a critical part of the classroom environment. Alphabet charts are helpful for all children and especially for English-language learners unfamiliar with the alphabet of their new language. It is also useful to have more than one alphabet chart for children to see and use. When I worked with a small group of kindergartners in their classroom, we sat at the back of the room near the bathroom. As the children drew and wrote in their journals, they made use of an alphabet chart that the teacher had taped to the bathroom door. As a result, they did not have to get up and walk to the other alphabet chart at the front of the room.

It is important to choose culturally responsive and authentic alphabet charts. Charts that use Indians for *I/i* and Eskimos for *E/e* or *I/i* (igloo) are examples of material that demeans cultural group affiliation. Teachers may want to make their own alphabet chart or ask children to paint and draw an alphabet. Another possibility for making one's own alphabet chart is to cut out the page for each letter of the alphabet from a book (you'll need two copies). For instance, Lois Ehlert's *Eating the Alphabet: Fruits and Vegetables from A to Z* is an excellent alphabet to use. The book's objects and letters, "SPINACH/spinach" for *S/s*, "TURNIP/turnip" for *T/t*, and "XIGUA/xigua" for *X/x* make for an attractive and informative display. It is also helpful, as in this book, for words to be in lower-case (*spinach*) and upper-case (*SPINACH*) for children to learn both.

It is also valuable to find and display alphabet charts in different languages for both bilingual classrooms and for English-language learners in English-medium classrooms. For children who speak languages that do not use an alphabet, such as Mandarin and Cantonese, which use characters, a list or chart of important strokes that form characters can be displayed.

Display Resource Materials and Information

Children make use of resource material displayed as visuals around the classroom. There are several advantages of posting large graphics listing strategies and reminders. A permanent display allows us to refer the children to the content of the list over the course of a school year; we don't have to rewrite it or look for it. I visited a primary-grade classroom that displayed a chart titled "What Good Readers Do." The large piece of chart paper listed helpful reminders and strategies for young readers: "practice reading a lot," "cover part of the word," "read everywhere around you." This kind of visible and accessible list or chart allows children to find their own information. Such visuals can be enhanced through pictures, photos, and vocabulary in multiple languages.

In another example of graphic displays of information, a classroom in Hawai'i displayed a map and chart titled, "*Ma hea mai kou 'ohana*/Where is your family from originally?" The children's family photographs were pinned to the world map to designate the children's areas of origin, and graphs to the side depicted the children's geographic and cultural origins. The map and the chart were clear and easily visible graphics that also integrated multiple curricular areas—languages, literacy, geography, math, and community building. The map and graphs provided a permanent visual display that children were able to access for class discussions and their projects.

A carefully designed and arranged classroom environment for literacy takes time, sensitivity, and thought. A well-designed literacy environment entices young children into the world of school literacy, and speaks to the literacy interests and experiences of teachers, children, and families. Colorful and inviting areas for literacy engagement, useful graphic displays and sources of information, flexible boundaries between activity and participation areas, and multilingual environmental print are just some of the critical elements that make for richly textured places for literacy in school.

SELECTING AND USING BOOKS

An essential factor in a successful literacy environment involves the selection and use of high-quality books for young children. This is critical for all children, and especially so for children who may not come to school with many book experiences. A well-run collection of books needs to function somewhat like a real library, with a varied permanent collection of books and a continual introduction of new books to stimulate children's interests. There are several important elements to consider in selecting and using books in a classroom environment.

Consider Children's Development and Memory

The first issue to consider involves matching books with where children are developmentally in terms of their overall growth and development. Their successful engagement with books is partly influenced by their emerging memories for what they have lived and experienced. And they can transfer these memories to books (and to one another) through opportunities for reading and looking at books that speak to their home, community, and school experiences. It is therefore helpful to create a varied collection of books in the classroom library and other literacy areas that speak to children's interests and developmental levels. This means that preschoolers within the 3–5-year-old range will react to books in some different ways; a 3-year-old and a 5-year-old, even in the same mixed-aged group or setting, will at times want different kinds of books. This is not to say that younger and older preschoolers need to be separated for book reading and read-alouds—they do not. Younger preschoolers will benefit from seeing and experiencing the book selection and ways of interacting of older preschoolers. And in turn, the older children can influence the literacy and books interests of the younger children.

Second, young children benefit from sophisticated books that might be seen as appropriate only for older children. For example, preschoolers and kindergartners need children's literature and storybooks as well as informational books on the ocean, space, volcanoes, holidays and celebrations, giraffes and elephants, artists and painters, musical instruments and the orchestra, architecture, and so on. Even if the children cannot read, they will understand and absorb information and knowledge from the pictures and photographs. To supplement what is not easily interpreted from these visuals, we can read portions of the text to give children an idea of the book's content and information.

Third, in thinking about book selection and children's literacy development, it is helpful to make a distinction between books for literacy engagement and books for actual reading development. Two separate goals are at issue: promoting an overall appreciation and involvement with reading and books and encouraging engagement in the more specific areas of reading knowledge. Children need both, and depending on their age and developmental capabilities, they need both kinds of books within an integrated, balanced literacy program.

An important way to link books for literacy enjoyment and those for reading knowledge is to offer books that children can commit to memory. These have an engaging story line, are liked by both preschoolers and kindergartners, and have a patterned text that lends itself to memorization. They speak to children's natural propensity for imitating sounds and words and to their talent for memorizing patterned text. Most children love to commit a favorite story or book to memory, and children even of preschool age rely on their knowledge of memorized texts to feel successful and competent in their earliest "reading" experiences. Examples of books that lend themselves to memorization and recitation from memory include John Archambault and Bill Martin's *Chicka Chicka Boom Boom* and Bill Martin and Eric Carle's *Brown Bear, Brown Bear, What Do You See?* and *Polar Bear, Polar Bear, What Do You Hear?* These books and others that have a distinctive rhythm and text pattern are also especially helpful for English-language learners in their becoming more familiar with English vocabulary and syntax.

Vary Sizes and Shapes

Babies and toddlers first come to know books through touching and smelling and trying to eat books; this is the developmental line that continues on through preschool and the primary grades. Preschoolers and kindergartners, then, need opportunities to physically experience books in varied sizes and shapes—big books, small books, flap books, board books, paperback and hardcover books, books that make sounds and flash lights, pop-up books, and books with puppets, animals, felt pieces, and other items to hold and move. The inclusion of varied sizes and shapes of books show children that books and literacy can come alive for them—books look and feel different, and children can read and interact with books according to their own individual interests.

There are particular advantages to making available to children multiple copies of big books. For example, preschoolers Joseph and Jeremiah looked at a big book of dinosaurs and pointed to an illustration of several dinosaurs. "I'm him! I'm him!" Joseph shouted. To which Jeremiah replied, "You can't be two of them." Shatani and Ashari joined the boys on the floor with a second copy of the same big book on dinosaurs. Shatani said, "I'm long neck. He's eating. Long necks eat trees." She turned to the boys and said, "Look, we got the long neck, too." This example shows how multiple copies of big books encourage social interaction and discussion.

Rethink Book Length and Text Complexity

When Kaili, my daughter, was in preschool, she loved looking at and listening to such different books as Margaret Wise Brown's *Goodnight Moon*, which has a short text and simple vocabulary, and Gary Soto's *Chato and the Party Animals*, a longer book with a more involved story line, some Spanish words, and more involved illustrations. This surprised me. In teaching preschoolers, and working on their language and literacy development, I had usually read and used shorter books typically thought of as developmentally appropriate for 3–5- year-olds. I discovered, though, that Kaili loved *Chato and the Party Animals* because of the complex illustrations; the large cast of characters, ranging from Chato to Novio Boy to the family of mice; the mix of Spanish and English vocabulary; the longish plot; and the story's continuation of certain characters from Gary Soto's *Chato's Kitchen*.

Kaili especially loved the lines from *Chato and the Party Animals* that read, "His tail began to swing to the rhythm. He felt the twinge of mambo in his hips." I would read, "His tail began to _____" and "He felt a _____," and Kaili would fill in the phrases with delight. Preschoolers are capable of interacting with long books, complex text and content, and sophisticated vocabulary if we create reading and learning formats that support children's close and intimate interaction with books. These formats include one-to-one and small-group book browsing and reading with young children, opportunities to talk and ask questions about the book *as it is being read*, the chance to touch and feel the book as children look for a favorite scene or point out a particular animal or character, and opportunities for children to talk in their first language to encourage engagement with the book.

Provide Culturally Relevant Books

Children's literature and nonfiction books are powerful sources for culturally relevant content and images. We should select books that contain broad and authentic representations of languages, culture, ethnicity, race, religion, and gender in their illustrations, language, and content. The children in the books need to look and talk like our students (and ourselves).

For instance, if we have African American children in our classrooms, a good proportion of the books need to speak to the experiences, interests, languages, and cultural and historical experiences of African American life. The books should also touch on such African American values and traditions as those pertaining to family, community, kinship, language, storytelling, literature, art, music, inventions, foods, historical events, and holidays and celebrations. The literacy materials also need to have narrators and characters that articulate the breadth of Englishes that African Americans speak, read, and write (see chapter 2). There are many excellent books that portray African American life with power and authenticity, and I list some at the close of this chapter. Varied and sophisticated books devoted to African American life benefit not only the literacy learning of African American children, but also everyone else in the class. Children of different ethnicities will learn and grow as readers and writers through experiencing books by African American authors who reveal the history, traditions, languages, and cultural lives of African Americans.

Include Multilingual Books

Bilingual learners and English-language learners benefit from access to books in more than one language. These include books that are written in two languages and those that are written in a range of different languages. Multilingual books build on children's oral language knowledge in different languages and promote biliteracy and even multiliteracy. For instance, Mehrnush, whom I introduced in chapter 1, is trilingual and triliterate in Farsi, English, and Spanish. As a third grader, Mehrnush has benefited from classroom literacy environments that support her cultural and linguistic identity and her multilingualism/multiliteracy knowledge. For children in the early stages of learning a second language, as Mehrnush was when she was in preschool and kindergarten, multilingual books are powerful resources for language and literacy learning. For example, bilingual books provide the full text in both languages on the same page. In a Spanish-English book, this can be helpful for Spanish speakers learning English, for English speakers learning Spanish, and for proficient, or nearly proficient, Spanish-English bilingual speakers. However, children in the early stages of reading in bilingual classrooms need monolingual books in their first language.

Bilingual books can be found in published bilingual reading series as well as children's picture books and informational books. Excellent examples of English-Spanish bilingual books are listed at the end of this chapter. Some bilingual books include the same text in two languages, such as in Jose Luis Orozco's *Diez deditos/Ten Little Fingers, and Other Play Rhymes and Action Songs from Latin America*, and Rebecca Emberley's *My Day/Mi día*. There are other books in which only part of the text is in another language. For example, in Alma Flor Ada's *I Love Saturdays y Domingos*, the majority of the text is in English, with selected words and phrases in Spanish. The story is about a girl who has two sets of grandparents, one of whom speaks English and the other Spanish. On one page, while the girl is with her English-speaking grandparents, the text reads, "One Saturday, Grandpa and Grandma play a movie about the circus for me on their VCR. 'I like the circus, especially the lions and tigers,' says Grandpa." On the opposite page, when the girl visits her Spanish-speaking grandparents, the text reads, *"Un domingo, Abuelito y Abuelita* take me to a real circus. *'Me encanta el circo, Abuelito'*—I say." Children can learn new English and Spanish vocabulary either by our pointing out the translation—"I like the circus" and *"Me encanta el circo"*—or by the children listening to the two languages and piecing together the translation from linking the action and the pictures.

Emphasize Vocabulary

Since children learn a great deal of their oral language vocabulary by age 4 or 5, books are a tremendous source for learning new words within varied syntactical constructions. Learning new vocabulary means that children learn new words and learn to connect language to books and to their experiences in the world. There are several key elements for promoting vocabulary growth. First, children need to connect words with objects and experiences. This is "vocabulary in action." For example, Amalia, a first grader receiving extra help at school for her reading, visited my house. She had read a book about hedgehogs at school but had never seen a hedgehog. At my house, she saw a small ceramic hedgehog in the backyard and exclaimed, "Oh so that's a hedgehog!" Amalia remembered the pictures of a hedgehog from her book and reconnected this memory with the hedgehog in my backyard.

Preschoolers and kindergartners also benefit from engaging storybooks with complex vocabulary and language. In Beatrix Potter's *The Tale of Squirrel Nutkin*, page 13 reads, "One autumn when the nuts were ripe, and the leaves on the hazel bushes were golden and green—Nutkin and Twinkleberry and all the other little squirrels came out of the wood, and down to the edge of the lake." This is only one sentence, but it is rich in vocabulary and English syntax. There is so much to discuss here with children. We can talk about what it means when nuts are "ripe," and talk about ripe bananas and ripe peaches and what it feels like when things are ripe versus when they are not. This can be related to trips we might make to the local grocery store for buying fruit, or the fruit that grows at different times of the year in a school garden. We can talk about what "golden and green" leaves would look like. Most young children know what green looks like, fewer recognize golden as a color, and even fewer will have an idea of golden and green together. So we can take a walk around the school and look at the autumn leaves or look at other books about autumn. "All the other little squirrels came out of the wood . . ." We can discuss other verbs for "came out of" such as *emerged* or *appeared*, that will get children to compare and contrast words.

In the phrase "down to the edge of the lake," we can point out the word *edge*, and connect this for our children "to where we line up at the edge of the playground," or "we use the edge of the ruler for writing lines," or the "edge of the blocks touched each other when we were building today in the block house." And both the ruler and the blocks can be shown to the children, reinforcing our verbal explanations with a concrete object.

So from only one line of a book, much rich vocabulary and language can be teased out. I have mentioned a range of ideas for extending and expanding children's vocabulary to show the language potential of complex, interesting text and books. Some of the teaching ideas, such as discussing what it means when nuts and bananas and peaches are "ripe" (or not ripe), can be accomplished in a 10-minute discussion with children during or after book reading. Then, the next day, we can write down the children's ideas and memories of that brief discussion. This will reinforce for the children the value of talking about language and vocabulary. Then, the next week, we can go on a field trip to the market to buy, touch, smell, and eat ripe fruit of various kinds. In this way, the one line from the *Squirrel Nutkin* can start with a brief discussion, extend into a whole-class brainstorm or language experience, and then extend yet again into a field trip and experiential activities with the fruit. Taking apart small pieces of rich and complex text, and focusing on vocabulary, can lead (quite spontaneously if we let ourselves go) to this kind of extended language/literacy/science/social studies project on nuts, fruits, and the idea of something being "ripe" or not.

The examples discussed above of extended explanations and demonstrations of vocabulary are particularly helpful for English-language learners, who need new vocabulary explained in varied linguistic and experiential contexts. In this way, they begin adding to their repertoire and see how and why words can have similar and different shades of meaning. For English-language learners, it is also helpful to make connections between the book's illustrations and photographs and the text's vocabulary. Since many English-language learners focus on the visuals in a book, this is critical for their English language growth. For instance, I read a version of *The Little Red Hen* with Jesus, a Spanish-speaking preschooler learning English. When I read the part about the red hen asking her friends to help her cut the wheat, Jesus stared at the picture of the wheat and asked, "Is this fire?" I looked at the wheat closely, and it did indeed look more like flames than wheat. I explained that it could be fire, since it did look like it, but it was actually called wheat, and I explained what that was.

When we select particular new words to focus on each time we read a book, children will have an accumulated understanding and memory for words over weeks and months. Much of children's vocabulary growth is not immediate; they need time to hear, repeat, use, and internalize new words in new literacy contexts. Repeated readings of the same books are thus particularly beneficial for increasing children's word knowledge. For example, William Steig's *Amos and Boris* contains sophisticated language for young children. Yet we can promote understanding of the book's words by breaking it down into bite-size pieces through repeated readings. One page reads, "One night, in a phosphorescent sea, he marveled at the sight of some whales spouting luminous water; and later, lying on the deck of his boat, gazing at the immense, starry sky, the tiny mouse Amos, a little speck of a living thing in the vast living universe, felt thoroughly akin to it all." The Spanish version of the same sentence reads, "Una noche, en un mar fosforescente, se maravilló al ver el chorro luminoso que arrojaban algunas ballenas: y más tarde, recostado sobre la cubierto de su bote contemplando el immenso cielo estrellado, el minúsculo ratón Amos, una pequeña pizca de cosa viviente en el vasto unviverso viviente, se sintió en completa armonia con el todo." Since we do not speak like this—the words and constructions in books often differ from those in our everyday language use—children need close attention to some key vocabulary and how the words are used.

For instance, we can focus on the single word *phosphorescent* in English and *fosforescente* in Spanish. This one word is enough for a day or more of exploration—we can pronounce the word, identify and count the letters, compare the letters and sounds of the word in English and Spanish, discuss what a phosphorescent sea might look like. These are all possibilities for focusing on one word that brings about a high level of word awareness and a memory for the text's language. In developmentally appropriate activities in which textual language is broken down into bite-size pieces, young children can pick up new words and begin hearing and using new words to express new thoughts, feelings, and ideas.

Even books with less complicated language than *Amos and Boris* and *Amos y Boris* provide material for vocabulary development and for fostering a memory for words. Examples of books with appropriate English vocabulary and repetitive, structured language and storylines include Nancy Tafuri's *Have You Seen My Duckling?* Eric Carle's *From Head to Toe*, Sue Williams's *I Went Walking*, and Nina Crews's *A High, Low, Near, Far, Loud, Quiet Story*. This last book is excellent for English-language learners. The photographs and the one-word-per-page format provide a good foundation for learning such important conversational words as *high* and *low*, *empty* and *full*, *outside* and *inside*. It is also a book that children can dramatize, putting a book *high* on the shelf or lying down on the rug and holding a bucket *low* to the ground as pictured in the book. The book also lends itself to the adding of other words with similar meanings. For instance, in looking at the double spread depicting *fast* and *slow*, children can describe what they look like when they run on the playground ("I run fast. I'm as quick as Michael Jordan"). This kind of "vocabulary extension" shows English-language learners subject-verb-adjective/adverb order in English syntax ("I run fast") and how simple sentences can be lengthened ("I'm as quick as Michael Jordan").

Selecting and using books are critical for establishing and maintaining an inviting, rich environment for literacy. Children need books that are developmentally appropriate, that are culturally responsive, and that can be used for both informal reading engagement and more formal learning-to-read activities. All young children, and especially English-language learners, need multicultural and multilingual books and other literacy resources that validate and support their multiple language backgrounds and the specific linguistic and cultural goals of the classroom and school setting. The particular design, organization, and collections of literacy materials in a classroom make impressions, conscious and unconscious, on children's literacy engagement and learning. Young children, anchored in the world of the senses and in exploration, create memories for words and books and literacy through intimate, close-in interaction with their immediate environment. They accumulate memories for what literacy can be, and what it can be used for, through associating reading and writing and talking with the particular worlds of our classrooms.

SUGGESTED ACTIVITIES

1. Look around your classroom. What do you like about your literacy environment and what would you like to change? Make a list of what you want to keep and what you want to change. Talk with your children and your colleagues to gain ideas. Implement a few changes in collaboration with colleagues and observe the effects on the children's literacy involvement and learning.
2. Examine the children's interaction and use of a literacy area over the course of a few or several weeks. Are all children gaining access to the area and making full use of the materials? For instance, are girls and boys using the library area? If so, what books are they reading and not reading? The children can help you in this research by keeping track of what they are reading (and not reading) and thus provide much food for discussion and changes in literacy routines.
3. Enlist the help of your children's families. Encourage them to bring in their books from their childhoods and their favorite books and literacy materials that they use and read now as adults, and get them to share their interests with the children and one another. Consider devoting an area of the classroom to literacy for the adults and families and solicit their ideas for making this happen.
4. Search out new books and materials for your English-language learners and multilingual speakers. What new titles can you find at your local library or in searching some of the book publishers and distributors listed in the Useful

Resources section at the back of this chapter? Once the books are purchased or borrowed, and put into use, observe how the children interact with the materials and how new vocabulary may appear in their conversation about books.

USEFUL RESOURCES

Literacy Environment

Carter, M., & Curtis, D. (2003). *Designs for living and learning: Transforming early childhood environments.* St. Paul, MN: Redleaf.

Diller, D. (2003). *Literacy work stations: Making centers work.* York, ME: Stenhouse.

Houle, A., & Krogress, A. (2001). The wonders of word walls. *Young Children, 56*(5), 92–95.

Schickendanz, J. A. (1993). Designing the early childhood classroom environment to facilitate literacy development. In B. Spodek & O. N. Saracho (Eds.), *Language and literacy in early childhood education: Yearbook in early childhood education* (pp. 141–155). New York: Teachers College Press.

Seefeldt, C. (2002). *Creating rooms of wonder: Valuing and displaying children's work to enhance the learning process.* Beltsville, MD: Gryphon House.

Xu Hong, S., & Rutledge, A. L. (2003). Kindergartners learn through environmental print. *Young Children, 58*(2), 44–51.

Selecting and Using Children's Books

Ada, A. F. (1989). *Language arts through children's literature: Using children's books to develop critical thinking and expression.* Emeryville, CA: Children's Book Press.

Ada, A. F. (2003). *A magical encounter: Latino children's literature in the classroom.* Boston, MA: Allyn & Bacon.

Bishop, R. S. (1990). Walk tall in the world: African American literature for today's children. *Journal of Negro Education, 59*(4), 556–565.

Cai, M., & Bishop, R. S. (1994). Multicultural literature for children: Towards a clarification of the concept. In A. H. Dyson & C. Genishi (Eds.), *The need for story: Cultural diversity in classroom and community* (pp. 57–71). Urbana, IL: National Council of Teachers of English.

Duke, N. K. (2003). Reading to learn from the very beginning: Information books in early childhood. *Young Children, 58*(2), 14–20.

Harris, V. (Ed.). (1993). *Teaching multicultural literature in grades K–8.* Norwood, PA: Christopher Gordon.

Rhoten, L., & Lane, M. (2001). More than abc's: The new alphabet books. *Young Children, 57*(2), 41–45.

Schön, I. (2000). Delightful books in Spanish for young children. *Young Children, 55*(1), 82–83.

Slapin, B., Seale, D., & Gonzales, R. (2000). *How to tell the difference: A guide to evaluating children's books for anti-Indian bias.* Berkeley, CA: Oyate.

Trelease, J. (1994). *The read-aloud handbook* (4th ed.). New York: Penguin.

Children's Books Cited in Chapter 3

Ada, A. F. (1980). *Abecedario de los animales*. Madrid: Espasa Calpe.

Ada, A. F. (2002). *I love Saturdays y domingos*. New York: Atheneum.

Archambault, J., & Martin, B. (1989). *Chicka chicka boom boom*. New York: Simon & Schuster.

Bang, M. (1983). *Ten, nine, eight*. New York: Greenwillow Books.

Bang, M. (1999). *When Sophie gets angry*. New York: Blue Sky Press.

Brett, J. (1989). *The mitten*. New York: Putnam.

Brown, M. W. (1939). *The noisy book*. New York: Harper & Row.

Brown, M. W. (1947). *Goodnight moon*. New York: HarperCollins.

Carle, E. (1969). *The very hungry caterpillar*. New York: HarperCollins.

Carle, E. (1987). *Have you seen my cat?* New York: Simon and Schuster.

Carle, E. (1997). *From head to toe*. New York: HarperCollins.

Carle, E., & Martin, B. (1991). *Polar bear, polar bear, What do you hear?* New York: Henry Holt.

Crews, N. (1999). *A high, low, near, far, loud, quiet story*. New York: Greenwillow.

Ehlert, L. (1989). *Eating the alphabet: Fruits and vegetables from a to z*. San Diego: Harcourt Brace.

Emberley, R. (1993). *My day/Mi día*. Boston: Little Brown.

Martin, B., & Carle, E. (1967). *Brown bear, brown bear, What do you see?* New York: Holt, Rinehart & Winston.

Orozco, J. L. (1997). *Diez deditos/Ten little fingers, and other play rhymes and action songs from Latin America*. New York: Dutton Children's Books.

Paek, M. (1988). *Aekyung's dream*. San Francisco: Children's Book Press.

Potter, B. (1903). *The tale of Squirrel Nutkin*. London: F. Warne.

Sendak, M. (1963). *Where the wild things are*. New York: Harper & Row.

Soto, G. (1995). *Chato's kitchen*. New York: Putnam.

Soto, G. (2000). *Chato and the Party Animals*. New York: Putnam.

Steig, W. (1971). *Amos and Boris*. New York: Farrar, Strauss, & Giroux.

Steig, W. (1992). *Amos y Boris*. New York: Farrar, Strauss, & Giroux.

Tafuri, N. (1984). *Have you seen my duckling?* New York: Greenwillow.

Williams, S. (1990). *I went walking*. San Diego: Harcourt Brace Jovanovich.

Young, E. (1989). *Lon Po Po: A Red-Riding Hood story from China*. New York: Philomel.

Additional Children's Books with African American Themes and Content

Crews, N. (1995). *One hot summer day*. New York: Greenwillow Books

Crews, N. (1998). *You are here*. New York: Greenwillow Books.

Cummings, P. (1991). *Clean your room, Harvey Moon!* New York: Bradbury Press.

Flourney, V. (1985). *The patchwork quilt*. New York: Dial Books.

Greenfield, E. (1988). *Under the Sunday tree*. New York: Harper & Row.

Greenfield, E. (1991). *Big friend, little friend*. New York: Writers and Readers, Black Butterfly Board Books.

Haskins, F. (1992). *Things I like about Grandma*. Emeryville, CA: Children's Book Press.

Isadora, R. (2002). *Peekaboo morning*. New York: G. P. Putnam's Sons.

Johnson, A. (1990). *Do like Kyla*. New York: Orchard Books.

Kuklin, S., with Swoopes, S. (2001). *Hoops with Swoopes*. New York: Sun/Hyperion.

Lester, J. (1988). *More tales of Uncle Remus: Further adventures of Brer Rabbit, Brer Fox, Brer Wolf, the Doodang, and other creatures*. New York: Dial Books.

McDermott, G. (1972). *Anansi the spider*. New York: Holt, Rinehart, & Winston.

Pinkney, S. (2000). *Shades of Black: A celebration of our children*. New York: Scholastic.

Smalls, I. (1992). *Jonathan and his mommy*. Boston: Little Brown.

Smith, C. R. (2002). *Perfect harmony: A musical journey with the Boys Choir of Harlem*. New York: Hyperion Books for Children.

Steptoe, J. (1997). *In Daddy's arms I am tall: African Americans celebrating fathers*. New York: Lee & Low.

Bilingual and Multilingual Books

Ada, A. F., & Zubizarreta, R. (Trans.). (1997). *The lizard and the sun: A folktale in English and Spanish /La lagarija y el sol*. New York: Bantam Doubleday Dell.

Brown, M. W. (1995). *Buenas noches luna*. Mexico: Sistemas Técnicos de Edición.

Canizares, S., & Moreton, D. (1998). *Frogs/Ranas*. New York: Scholastic.

Chin, C. (1993). *China's bravest girl: The legend of Hua Mu Lan/Chin kuo ying hsiung Hua Mulan*. Emeryville, CA: Children's Book Press.

Cruz Martinez, A. (1991). *The woman who outshone the sun: The legend of Lucia Zenteno/ La mujer que brillaba aún más que el sol: La leyenda de Lucía Zenteno*. San Francisco: Children's Book Press.

De Zutter, H. (1993). *Who says a dog goes bow-bow?* New York: Doubleday Book for Young Readers.

Ehlert, L. (1992). *Moon rope/Un lazo a la luna*. San Diego: Harcourt Brace Jovanovich.

Feder, J. (1995). *Table-chair-bed: A book in many languages*. New York: Ticknor & Fields.

Hinojosa, T. (2002). *Cada niño/Every child: A bilingual songbook for kids*. El Paso, TX: Cinco Punto Press.

Murphy, J. (1995). *Five minutes' peace*. London: Magi.

Reiser, L. (1998). *Tortillas and lullabies/Tortillas y cancioncitas*. New York: Greenwillow Books.

Robles, A. (2003). *Lakas and the Manilatown fish/Si lakas at ang isdang Manilatown*. San Francisco: Children's Book Press.

Rodriguez, L. (2001). *Abc zoo/Abecedario zoológico*. Venezuela: Playco Editores.

Rohmer, H. (1989). *Uncle Nacho's hat /El sombrero del tío Nacho*. Emeryville, CA: Children's Book Press.

Williams, S. (1995). *Sali de paseo*. San Diego: Harcourt Brace Jovanovich.

Chapter 4

The Alphabet, Reading, and Books

Mr. Meier: What are letters for?
Ariel (preschooler): You put them in the book!

TEACHING AND LEARNING QUESTIONS

1. What does it mean to have knowledge about the alphabet? How necessary is such knowledge for literacy involvement and learning to read?
2. What is potentially challenging for English-language learners trying to learn the alphabet for English literacy?
3. How can we teach children alphabetic knowledge and also promote life-long passions and memories for literacy?
4. What is an effective format for small-group literacy work and play?

THE ALPHABET AND CHILDREN'S READING

Many of our memories for literacy link back to our earliest reading and literacy experiences. For those of us who grew up learning to read and write in a language that uses an alphabet, we may have quite particular memories of learning an alphabet song, memorizing letter names, and engaging in activities in which we matched letters with their corresponding sounds. As noted in the Introduction of this book, attention to learning the alphabet as a key ingredient in learning to read is emphasized in current literacy standards and curricula. Yet, as I argued earlier, while a focus on the alphabet is helpful and beneficial, it is not the sole foundation for enjoyable literacy engagement and successful literacy achievement. We need, then, to see children's knowledge of the alphabet as integrated with such other key elements as the use of high-quality children's literature, dictation and the language experience approach, art and music, project work, and writing.

The English Alphabet and Sound-Symbol Relationships

The Alphabet as a Symbol System

As a symbol system, the letters of the alphabet used in English represent words that in turn refer to almost everything that makes up our world. In considering children's understanding of oral and written language in English as a symbol system, it is helpful to consider the Russian psychologist Lev Vygotsky's view of language as a two-tiered system of symbols. The first level, the words we use to denote our worlds, is a first-order symbolic system. First-order symbolization refers to language at just one level of abstraction or symbolization. For example, the linguistic labels of *dog* and *cat* that refer to particular four-legged creatures are only one step away from the objects they refer to. And it is quite arbitrary that these animals are called *dog* and *cat* when they could be known by some other name in English. (And they are called something quite different in Spanish, Chinese, French, and other languages). When children are toddlers, they somehow sense this first-order symbolism when they call dogs "bow wows" and cats "meows," and we all know what the children are referring to.

Second-order symbolism refers to language as a symbol or representation of something two steps away from the real thing. For example, when children read and write the words *dog* and *cat*, they use the names of the animals (the words *dog* and *cat*) *and* the written symbols of d-o-g and c-a-t to denote the real animals. Reading and writing *dog* and *cat*, then, involve a second-order or twice-removed level of symbolization. For many children, moving from first- to second-order symbolization is a big developmental jump. It can be akin to making the move from crawling to walking and from babbling and cooing to saying actual words and phrases. Preschoolers and kindergartners exhibit a wide range of experience with and understanding of the alphabet as a system of symbols. For example, Leilani, a preschooler, interchangeably calls written letters and numerals "letters" and "numbers." They are both the same to her because at the moment they are lumped into the conceptual pile of "symbols," or some word standing for some object. Later on, as Leilani explores the forms and functions of letters and numerals (and understands that letters make up words and ideas and that numerals refer to numbers and mathematics), she will begin differentiating these kinds of symbols.

English-language learners need support with both first- and second-order symbolization in English. These children are in the process of mastering first-order language learning (English vocabulary and the placement of these words within English syntactical structures) *and* applying this first-order knowledge to second-order symbolization in reading and writing. This is a tall order in a first language, and it becomes even more complicated and involved in a second or third. English-language learners, then, need literacy activities that integrate first-order and second-order symbolization with the English alphabet, vocabulary, and syntax.

The Alphabet: Letters and Sounds

The English alphabet consists of 26 letters that in combination with one another serve as second-order symbols. When the alphabet in English is written and becomes text or print, the challenge is to read or decode the meanings that the combinations of letters (that is, words) denote. *Decode* refers to the process of taking apart, or breaking down, the particular letter combinations that form words, which in turn form phrases and sentences and whole texts. This is one of the central challenges for children when they are learning to read and write. They need to make the developmental jump—a process that can include a range of cognitive, linguistic, social, and cultural factors—from using oral language to interpreting this same language in written form. The challenge is one of understanding and using a second-order symbol system. And for a young child of preschool or kindergarten age, the jump from saying *cat* and *dog* and reading/decoding c-a-t and d-o-g in text takes time, patience, and expert guidance on our part.

Although it is often posited this way, the process of understanding and using the alphabet as a symbol system in reading and writing is not entirely a process of matching letters with their corresponding sounds (often referred to as sound-symbol correspondences). Just as when we read out loud we need to know how to recognize the array of sound-symbol combinations in English to say a word out loud, so too must children *if* we want them to read out loud. But to read successfully, we don't necessarily need to know the sounds that letters and letter combinations make. For example, some deaf children and deaf adults learn to read and write and communicate through written English, with skill and complexity, without hearing or producing the sounds that letters can make. And when we as adults read out loud, we often stumble over decoding or pronouncing words—we may be able to recognize the word as a whole visually and know what it means, but not be able to accurately decode the word out loud. We need to be careful, then, to avoid an overreliance on oral reading in early reading instruction for young children.

Understanding and Using the Alphabet: Developmental Considerations

Preschoolers and kindergartners can exhibit what can appear to be conflicting or not yet solidified knowledge about the alphabet as a symbol system. They are often looking for multiple ways to understand the alphabet that make sense to them, although this may appear to us as haphazard and inconsistent. For instance, I worked with Shartisha in January of her kindergarten year on recognizing the word *the* in our books and in our dictation and writing. One day Shartisha pointed to *the* in the title of a book, and then said, "T-h-e," as she moved her index finger across the printed word, going backward from right to left: e-h-t. A week later, we again looked for *the* in our words. We were reading a book, and Shartisha eagerly pointed to "The" and said, "T-h-e." And just 20 minutes later on that same day, Shartisha found another *the*, pointed to the *e*, and said, "Emile [another child in our group] has an *e*," pointed to the *h* and said, "I have an *h* in my name," and then pointed to the *t* and said, "My sister has a *t* in her name." Her sister's name is Tiffany. On another occasion, Shartisha looked at a name card with her teacher's name, Kim, and pointed to the *K* and the *i* and said, "Tea-cher," one syllable each for *K* and *i*. She then pointed to the *m* in *Kim* and said, "Kim!" In this last example, Shartisha continues to experiment with putting it all together—orchestrating her still not solid knowledge of syllables, letters, words, and sounds as encapsulated in the alphabet.

In another example, I worked with Aleya, a Spanish-speaking kindergartner learning English, who pointed at the title of a book, *At the Zoo*, and said, "Hip po patomus." Underneath the title there was a picture of a hippopotamus. She said "Hip" while she pointed to "At," said "po" while pointing to "the," and said "patomus" while pointing to "Zoo." Aleya combined the picture, the words of the title, the syllables, and the alphabet all in one! In another example, Marcos, another Spanish-speaking kindergartner, would recite the alphabet song in English and then place small plastic letters in alphabetic order. Just as some young children think that "lmnop" is one letter, Marcos saw the *and* in the phrase *x, y, and z* as a symbol and a letter to denote. He put down *y* and then said, "And z," then put down the *z* and said, "We need another *z*." He interpreted the *and* from the alphabet song as another letter and decided there should be another *z*, which makes perfect sense. He is counting each letter and word from the alphabet song as something to be represented in his plastic letter array. Marcos is correct in terms of matching an oral language symbol or item with what he considers the correct corresponding visual representation. He certainly understands the idea of symbols, though he needs more experience matching the letter names (from the song, for instance) with what the letters look like.

Learning the letter names and matching these names to the letter shapes can also be a challenge for children. For example, Julian, a kindergartner, picked up a lower-case *v* (a plastic letter). He wasn't sure which letter it was. I pointed to a *y*, to see if he knew that letter and would then remember the *v*. "A bigger case *y*?" he asked. Julian sees that the *v* is part of a *y*, though he is still unclear about the letter names for each. In another instance, I asked Alma, a Spanish-speaking kindergartner learning English, how she identified an upper-case *M*. "*M* is like a crown [that is, the top of the letter]. I learned it from my mom." Her mother's suggestion for visualizing an *M* made good developmental sense for Alma; and so I copied this visual clue to use with other children.

In helping children to recognize and read their earliest words, it is common for literacy teachers to focus on the initial letter (*t*) or letter combinations (*th*) in a word. This makes sense, since English is read from left to right and we often need to focus on the first letter(s) of each word. But this is *not* always useful for children. First, there are children who can read the entire word or at least the first few letters of a word and so do not need to focus only on the initial letter sound. It is helpful to notice this quickly in individual children, so that we don't waste their time in only focusing on initial letter sounds. Second, focusing on the first sound usually means focusing on the first letter that we see; and this is not always accurate or helpful. For example, with two-letter combinations such as *tr* and *bl* as in *truck* and *black*, the first sound is not /tuh/ or /buh/ but something closer to /truh/ and /bluh/, since the first two letters are combined to make a new set of sounds. This mistaking of two or more letters at the beginning of the word also confuses children when we try to rhyme words such as *black* and *back*, which are not exact rhymes, but are near rhymes.

Third, there are children who naturally look for and hear sounds in parts of words other than the initial letter. They are able to match a letter with its corresponding sound, but it may not be in the initial position. I worked with Marcos (mentioned above) on identifying letter names and sounds. I asked him "about a word or name for *Ii*," and Marcos replied, "Miguel." He was correct, since he gave a name with an *i* sound. If I had asked him only for a word or name that started with *I*, then he would have been incorrect and it would have decreased his opportunities for finding *is* at the beginning, middle, and end of a word or name. When I asked him to identify a word with an *x* in it, Marcos replied "Fox," and crossed his two index fingers to make an *x*. Again, he had found a word that did not start with the letter I wanted and expected, but a word with the letter in a different position.

Fourth, we can overemphasize the separation of letter sounds and letter names in developmental opposition to children's interests in putting the two together. For instance, I asked Marcos to identify an *s* and give a word or name with *s* in it. "Fish," he replied and made a swimming motion for a fish for added nonverbal emphasis. The letter *s*, with its customary sound /sss/, is lost in *fish*, and instead sounds more like /shuh/ when coupled with an *h*. So again Marcos was correct; he had found a word with an *s*, though it was not a word—such as *sat* or *pass*—that I expected at all.

Fifth, it is important to remember how literal and concrete young children, especially English-language learners such as Marcos, are in learning letter-sound knowledge. For example, I asked Marcos to identify the sound for *z*, and he replied, "Zuuhhh, zuuhhh. For sleeping. For snoring." The sound that *z* makes is the sound of someone snoring. He could have said, "Zebra," but the snoring sound is even more concrete and literal because he can hear the snoring, visualize the sound-action of snoring, and connect this association with the letter. This process of association helps Marcos build up a memory for linking sounds and letters in a new language.

Alphabetic Knowledge and Reading: A Few Caveats

There are a few central caveats to teaching the alphabet as the one and only precursor to reading development. First, some children do not learn the alphabet (that is, all the letter names and sounds) and yet still learn to read. I have known preschoolers who could not recognize all the letters of the alphabet, let alone know the corresponding sounds, but who recognized some words and could read them out loud and silently. These children somehow bypass the process of matching letters with corresponding sounds, and go right for the whole word, seeing patterns in words and written language. So not all children need extensive alphabetic- and phonemic-awareness activities; it is not so much that they already have it, but rather have already bypassed much of this process.

Second, there are children who know the sounds that letters make and can read some words, but still cannot identify all the names for the letters. This happened to me as an adult learning Spanish. I could read simple books out loud because I had learned the sound-symbol correspondences in Spanish, but at the time I did not know all the names of the letters in the Spanish alphabet. I really only needed to know them if I wanted to spell a word, and my tutor said the letters according to their Spanish names. As it happened for me, children will also eventually learn the letter names, and so it makes little sense to hold back reading experiences until all 26 letter names are mastered.

A third caveat, touched on earlier, involves an overreliance on oral reading as the *only* path to reading development. Not all children read well out loud all the time; some children need to read on their own quietly, as they sound out possible sound-symbol relationships internally and silently move their lips and mouths to form sounds. One day, Alexis, a kindergartner, read a book with the sentence "Dad is reading" and a picture of a man sitting and looking at an open book. Alexis read, "Dad is . . ." and then paused; I said, "Reading," and Alexis looked at me and said, "But the dad doesn't have his mouth open." Alexis, like many children, has come to associate reading only with reading out loud.

POTENTIAL CHALLENGES OF THE ENGLISH ALPHABET FOR ENGLISH-LANGUAGE LEARNERS

A number of aspects of alphabetic knowledge are potentially problematic for all young children, and especially for English-language learners new to important sound and symbol aspects of English.

What's Potentially Problematic

First, not all letters in the English alphabet are created equal; some are more powerful than others. Tom Prince, a primary-grade reading teacher, believes that the letter *Yy* is the most influential letter in the alphabet. It can act as a consonant and a vowel. For example, it acts as a consonant in *yellow* and *yard* and *yippee*. It acts as a vowel in *vying* and *my* and *already*, where it makes more than one kind of vowel sound (a long *i* vowel sound in *my* and a long *e* in *already*). It can also be paired with other vowels and produce different vowel sounds such as in *vying* (where the *y* sounds like a long *i*) and *play* (where the *ay* sounds like a long *a*). Further, *y* can come in front of suffixes such as –*ing* as in *playing* and *buying*, and so children need to recognize where the *y* is in the word and recognize the word and its suffix. Further, visually, the letter *Yy* contains the letter *Vv* in the top part of the letter, and children do confuse a *Yy* with a *Vv* on the basis of their visual similarities.

A second challenge for English-language learners is that certain letter names in English can be confusing. For example, when I give a letter-identification assessment to kindergarten-aged English-language learners, there are several letters that prove problematic for the children. Some children find the letter *c* confusing because they think that a corresponding word that starts with *c* should be *see.* This makes sense, since they hear a soft *c* or /sss/ sound in the letter name for *c*, /see/. Children also confuse *e* and *i*, especially when one of these begins a word. For example, Alejandra looked at an *i* and said, "*I* for *eyeballs*!" According to her logic, she is correct; the letter name for *i* is pronounced just like the long *i* sound in *eyeball*. In another example, Emile looked at Itanya's name, which he pronounced as /eetanya/, and asked me, "How come she don't got no *e* on her name?" Some of the children in their class pronounced her name as /eetanya/ and some pronounced it as /ihtanya/, so like Alejandra, it made sense for Emile to wonder about the letter *i* sounding more like the letter *e*—which, according to its name, should always sound like a long *e*.

Some children also find *Ff* and *Mm* confusing, especially if we introduce these two letters with an emphasis on a hidden vowel sound in front of the consonant, as in /eff/ for *Ff* and /emm/ for *Mm*. In these instances, children can mistake the actual sound for *Ff* or *Mm* as a letter or word starting with an *e*, which really would start such words as *empty* and *enter*. In another instance of confusion, children mistake the sound for *Ww* as something that starts with a /duh/ since the name of the letter is /duhbuhl yoo/, when it actually starts with a /whuh/ sound as in *water* and *witch*. Jon, an English-language learner from Eritrea, gave the sound of /duh/ for *w* during an assessment of letter names and sounds in February of his kindergarten year. Another child, Jasmin, just said, "That's a hard one!" when I asked her for the sound that *w* makes.

The letter *Xx* can also confuse children. For instance, *x* makes different sounds in *xylophone* and *ax*. (Further, for some speakers of African American English, *ask* can be pronounced like /aks/.) In a kindergarten class, there was a boy named Xavier, and all the children pronounced his name /ehks-zavier/, which made the *x* sound like it began with an *e*. In yet another kindergarten class, there was a child named Xenia, whose name sounded like /zen-ya/, with the *x* in *xylophone*. Sometimes the children used her name as an example of the sound /ks/ (as in *ax*) and also for the sound /zeh/ (as she pronounced her name).

For English-language learners a third challenge is that many letters in English simply do not make just one sound, as some letter-sound identification assessments might imply. For example, the letter *Aa* can make more than one sound, as in its different sounds in *bat*, *ball*, and *acorn*. The letter *Ee* also makes different sounds, as in *egg*, *level*, *some*, *new*, *used*, *the*, and *person*. These and other vowels change in sound because of their position within words and the particular construction of the words. English consonants also vary in their corresponding sounds. For example, the letter *Gg* makes different sounds either standing alone or in combination with other letters as in *gnarled*, *go*, *enough*, *gist*, *big*, *giant*, and *huge*. The same letter can also make two or more different sounds within the same word, as in *level*, *else*, *language*, *rewrite*, *area*, *entitled*, and *vantage*.

Fourth, a single letter in English rarely retains its discrete sound when placed in combination with other letters in a word. So if we overteach the value of pulling apart (e.g., the discrete sounds of /deh/ /ah/ /guh/ from *dog*) or putting sounds together (e.g., /deh/ and /ah/ and /guh/ to say *dog*), then we do not really teach children that a word has its own distinct sound composition. For example, when *dog* is read as a one-word entity, then it does not sound like the separate sounds of /deh/and /ah/ and /guh/. This is because once the letters are combined to form a word, the word is no longer a set of discrete sounds but rather becomes a whole sound-symbol entity. This does not mean, of course, that discrete sounds cannot be teased apart within the words, but that overteaching this practice can give children the mistaken impression that this is what reading is. And it is not.

Language-Specific Differences: English and Spanish

It is helpful to have some basic knowledge of differences between languages to support the early alphabetic and reading knowledge of English-language learners. In taking the case of English and Spanish, essential aspects of the alphabets—letter names, individual sounds, sound combinations, word stress, and so on—of each language are helpful for understanding possible points of confusion for children.

First, flexibility in the assessment and observation of children's alphabetic knowledge helps to give a clearer picture of their current developmental understanding. Often, in observing children's letter and sound knowledge, I write out the letters of the alphabet to include the children's names, and ask the children for names of family and friends that might include (not necessarily start) a particular letter. Alejandra, a Spanish-speaking kindergartner, said "g" for the letter *g* and then added, "[G for] Gabriel, my cousin's name." English-language learners whose native language is Spanish may also give examples of letter names and sounds in both Spanish and English. For instance, Alejandra identified the letter *j* as *hota*, as in the Spanish letter name for *j*, and said, "[J for] Julian, in my class." For *n*, she said "m" (confusing it with *m* as other children do) but then said, "Nicholas [for something that started with *n*].

When I worked with Juanita, she said "gato" for *c*—she most likely thought of the English *cat* for *c* but it came out as *gato* (*cat*). In another instance, Jesus said "b" and "bear" for the letter *p*. Jesus and other children learning English are still working out the challenge of differentiating the somewhat similar sounds that *b* and *p* can make. In English, *p* and *b* are both pronounced in close physical proximity in the mouth and with the tongue, whereas in Spanish the two are a little farther apart, as the *b* and *p* and *v* (as in *bueno* and *papa* and *vamos*).

One of the most vexing aspects of English for English-language learners is the set of exceptions to sound-symbol patterns and regularities in English. For instance, words such as *was* and *said* and many others do not follow a regular pattern of sound-symbol correspondence. This is not as prevalent in Spanish, where vowel sounds, for instance, are more consistent. The vowel sound *i* in Spanish usually sounds like /ee/ as in the Spanish *sin* or *mis*. In English, in contrast, *i* can contribute to all the different sounds in *hit*, *hike*, *insufficient*, *find*, *strategies*, and *piece*. This difference influences how children learn to read in Spanish. Children are often taught to read in Spanish by learning the alphabet and then a specific sequence of syllables: *ma, me, mi, mo, mu; pa, pe, pi, po, pu; sa, se, si, so, su*, and so on. So Spanish speakers learning English need a different kind of support to help them recognize and hear the different sound-letter-syllable patterns in English. Their eyes and ears are attuned to different language patterns.

English also has more possibilities for individual consonants and consonant combinations to stand for multiple sounds than is found in Spanish. For example, Jemina said "elephant" as a word containing the sound that *f* makes. Of course, *ph* in this English word does sound like the *f* in Spanish, and *elephant* is spelled in Spanish as *elefante* (there is no written *ph* in Spanish). So at some point in her English-literacy development, Jemina will have to learn that *ph* also makes the sound of the letter *f*. In another instance of learning the sound-symbol complexities of English, Jemina said "Jemina" for the sound that *e* makes, "Jemina" for the sound that *h* makes, and "Jemina" yet again for the sound that *J* makes. Jemina's response of her own name for e makes some sense—she might be hearing the long e sound in her name because of the sound of the Spanish letter *i* (/ee/). Jemina is almost correct, again, in giving her name for the sound of *h*, since the Spanish *J* sounds like the letter *h* in *horse* or *hot*. In the third instance, she gives her name for the sound of *J*; and this too makes sense, since this is the correct letter for the English letter *J*. So Jemina is in a beginning stage of making developmental sense of English and Spanish sound-symbol knowledge.

Learning about the alphabet can be part of promoting memories for books and for the process of learning how to read. Alphabetic knowledge is essentially a long process of learning about the alphabet as a symbol system, in which the sounds and words that we use every day are transposed into a written language. As children move from oral to written language, they take a journey along a continuum of understanding language as a system of symbols. Although knowledge of the alphabet—identifying letter names and letter sounds, and which combinations of letters make which sounds—is critical for early reading development, it is not the sole factor. As such, teaching about the alphabet need not be the exclusive focus for young children's early reading experiences. For English-language learners, the alphabet in English may pose particular challenges—ranging from identifying letter names to understanding English sound patterns—and so English-language learners need specific support in fostering memories for using a new alphabet in a new language.

PROMOTING EARLY LITERACY THROUGH A SMALL-GROUP FORMAT

A small-group literacy format provides an excellent way to observe, interact, and guide young children in their earliest explorations of the alphabet, putting letters and sounds together and reading both for enjoyment and for reading development. Working in small groups provides us with time and energy for observing and recording the children's literacy play and work and allows children more opportunities for literacy participation. This structure is also conducive to one-to-one interactions between teachers and children and also between the children themselves. As compared with whole-group activities, a small-group format benefits English-language learners by giving them more time and opportunities to speak and for discussion, more assistance in recalling and learning English vocabulary, and more opportunities to get physically closer to us and to books and other visuals.

In working with small groups, a four-part format works well:

1. *Opening Routine*—use of name clapping, songs, finger rhymes, and other language play to provide oral language foundation for literacy activities
2. *Read-alouds*—reading of high-quality multicultural, multilingual children's books followed by discussion or activity
3. *Personal Journals*—children draw, write, and dictate in their own personal journals as they talk and interact with peers and adults
4. *Informal Book Browsing and Sharing*—children choose books from the read-alouds or classroom libraries for independent reading and sharing with peers and adults

This basic format allows us to work both with a small group to build a sense of a literacy community and also to work with children individually. One of the greatest pitfalls of whole-class teaching is that by definition each child does not receive individual attention from us.

I first discuss the opening routine, in the following section, then I turn to the read-alouds and informal book browsing and sharing. The discussion on personal journals is found in chapter 5.

Opening Routine: Language "Warm-Ups" for Literacy

Name Chanting

Going around our circle of four to six children, we all chant and clap our names. The children always delight in hearing their names repeated in rhythmic unison. They approach the activity as being fun as they listen for their own name, but they don't know that we are really focusing on the distinct sounds and rhythm of each child's name. "Da-li-sa, Da-li-sa, Da-li-sa," and "An-gel, An-gel, An-gel" as we clap together. This kind of attention to syllables helps English-language learners begin to segment the names into small chunks, or syllables, which helps them to see and hear the internal boundaries in names and words.

Language Breakers

I then lead the group in another language "warm-up," in which the children quickly learn nonverbal language and the gestures that accompany the words:

- "Hug yourself once [as children give themselves a hug!], hug yourself twice, hug yourself three times."
- "Yay me [children give themselves a double thumbs-up], yay you [turn to a neighbor and give that child a double thumbs-up], yay you, yay you."
- "Double flex [raise both fists in the air like an athlete], flex down [have one fist and arm up and the other down], flex up [reverse the fists and arms]."
- "Make a house [children place their hands together by intertwining their fingers and place them in their lap]."

I use this language breaker at any time during our small group session when I feel the children need to be refocused. It is much more valuable for children's language learning if such refocusing strategies make use of oral and nonverbal language that children can participate in rather than there being teacher directives simply to "stop talking" or "pay attention."

Alphabet Song

We sing the alphabet song and snap our fingers and clap to each letter. I also pause at certain points in the song so children can see how the song can have natural breaks and as a way to allow children more time to experience the song's rhythm and remember the letter order:

"a, b, c, d, e, f, g" (pause)
"h, i, j, k, l, m, n, o, p" (pause)

"q, r, s, t, u, v" (pause)
"w, x, y, and, z, z, z" (pause)
"now I know my abc's, next time won't you sing with me, me, me"
    (as we point to ourselves with our thumbs)

Then, depending on the children's capabilities, I continue with the two-letter *me* to include other two-letter words (such as *go* and *is*) as we touch "our two ears and our two eyes and our two knees" and so on. We touch a knee and say *g* and then touch the other knee and say *o* for *go*. This is helpful for English-language learners, who benefit from this playful repetition, using parts of the body.

Name Cards

I make a pile of name cards out of all the children's first names in their class or preschool. I also add my name ("Mr. Meier") and that of the children's teacher. (For children with more than one name—e.g., one Chinese and one English—each name can be put on a side of the name card and shared with the children. The Chinese name can be written in Chinese characters.) Although I am only working in small groups, we read all the children's names in the class or preschool. I write each child's name on a small piece of thick paper in magic marker, and for kindergartners I write the first letter in a different color from that of the rest of the letters. I also ask each child to add a sticker to his or her name card. This helps personalize the name cards and also serves as a visual cue for remembering the names. For example, children say, "Oh, that's David because he has a train sticker."

There are a number of ways to use the name cards. First, they can be used for copying and writing, which I describe later in the third section discussing the small-group format. Second, the name cards can be used as flash cards: As I say (looking at Mariella's name card), "M [the letter] for _____" and let the children supply Mariella's name or give the first sound of *Mmmmmm* and let the children complete her name. Sometimes, there are certain names that almost all the children easily recognize—such as Xavier or Xenia or Zena or other names that start with *X* or *Z*. If most of the children, though, are unfamiliar with recognizing one another's names, I then read almost all of the name, "Mar-i-el . . ." and wait for the children to supply the missing *la*. There are other possibilities for using the name cards:

- Say "Good morning to _____" and supply the child's name from the card. Then when we go through the names again as we put the cards away, say, "Good-bye to _____." This way we read and hear each child's name twice.
- Spread out the name cards one by one as the children place all the names that begin with *B* in one pile and so on. We can then count

and find out which letter has the most names and which one has the least.

- Look for "twins," or repeated letters, such as the double *ll* in *Mariella* and the two *r*s in *Larry*. Over time, children learn to see these twin letters not only on the name cards, but also in names and words around their classrooms and in books.

- Ask the children, "How did you know that was Mariella's name?" And often the children respond, "I saw the *M*" or "I remembered her name has two *l*s in it."

Read-Alouds and Informal Book Browsing: Using High-Quality Children's Books

Alphabet Books

Alphabet books can be used solely to teach recognition of letters and their sounds, but often excellent alphabet books teach content, or tell an inventive story, or both. Examples of alphabet books that focus on rich content and sophisticated language include Ashley Bryan's *ABC of African American Poetry*, Lois Ehlert's *Eating the Alphabet: Eating the Fruits from A to Z* (mentioned in Chapter 3), and George Shannon's *Tomorrow's Alphabet*. *The ABC of African American Poetry* features important people and aspects of African American life. The *H* page features Eloise Greenfield and a poem that begins, "Harriet Tubman didn't take no stuff . . ." The *R* page is for "Black American Spiritual," and the poem begins, "Roll Jordan roll . . ." Children, then, acquire important knowledge about African American life as they listen to the poetry and hear the sounds for the particular letters.

Tomorrow's Alphabet simply and elegantly shows how certain objects transform appearance and shape over varied periods of time. "J is for pumpkin—tomorrow's Jack-o-Lantern." "R is for grapes—tomorrow's raisins." "U is for stranger—tomorrow's us." Leilani, a preschooler who does not like alphabet books, finally agreed to let me read this book, and after hearing the *R* page, she exclaimed, "I didn't know raisins come from grapes!" These kinds of content-rich alphabet books introduce important knowledge to young children as they also learn sound-symbol correspondences.

At the end of the chapter I provide a list of additional recommended alphabet books.

"Sound" and Rhythm Books

Young children, both those listening to books in their native language and others experiencing the sounds of a new second language, benefit from books that focus on various sounds. These kinds of books provide links to children's earliest language experiences as infants when they learned to follow and internalize the language sounds of their new environments.

Andrea and Brian Pinkney's *Shake, Shake, Shake* is a simple book for preschoolers in which an adult uses a *shekere* (a percussion instrument from West Africa) in a playful, musical way with two young children. "Roll it in your hands, feel it shake, shake, shake" (pp. 5–6), says the text. The simple imagined movement of the *shekere* and its imagined sounds provide young children who are listening to the text and looking at the pictures with a simple musical experience via a book. The book also lends itself to movement, as children can hold their own real or pretend *shekeres* and dance and move along with the characters in the book.

Margaret Wise Brown's *The Noisy Book* is a wonderful early text that focuses on the sounds of the city. It has a story line that children enjoy ("One day a little dog named Muffin got a cinder in his eye" and needs a bandage to cover the one eye) and sophisticated vocabulary ("cinder," "shine," "coal car," "empty," "hoofs") relating children's senses of sound and sight. The book provides excellent oral language extensions for English language learners. For example, the dog hears, "Bzzzzzzzzz bzzzzzzzz a bee, Swishhhhh swishhhh car wheels, Chirp chirp a bird, Meoww meoww a pussycat, Patter patter patter patter people's feet, Flippity flap flap flap an awning in the wind." Just as Muffin must imagine what these *sounds look like*, because of his bandage over one eye, children match the sounds with their corresponding objects.

Preschoolers love Helen Oxenbury's *Tickle, Tickle*, enjoying the rhythm and sounds of the text—"Squelch, squelch, in the mud, splish, splash, scrub-a-dub"—and the simple pictures help children match certain sounds with their corresponding actions. As Leilani, our preschooler said, "I really like 'splish, splash, scrub-a-dub' because it is a funny word." Young children pay attention to phrases in text when the language is inventive and inviting, as in this book. Pat Cummings's *My Aunt Came Back* is also a favorite for its sounds and rhyming story of a young girl's aunt who brings her gifts from faraway places: "My aunt came back from Bucharest." The last word on the page is the rhyming "vest." Kindergartners can also enjoy this book by identifying the rhyming words.

Michael Hague's *Teddy Bear, Teddy Bear* has a rhyming, moving text that young children can easily imitate and commit to memory after only a few readings. "Teddy Bear, Teddy Bear" starts each page of text; and English-language learners benefit from matching the book's vocabulary ("show your shoe," "go upstairs," "turn off the light") with the corresponding actions depicted in the pictures. In Chapter 1, I described how Han, an English-language learner, described "turning off the light" as "*tsskkkk*," or the sound that the pull chain makes when you turn off a lamp. *Teddy Bear*, which depicts the language and action of turning off the light, will help Han learn the vocabulary (*light, off, turn, the*) and place these words in correct English syntax (*turn off the light*). Han and other English-language learners will also benefit from physically acting and dramatizing the actions described in the book's text and pictures. It is an excellent book to use at story time; having the children stand and move as the book is read is a good technique.

Bilingual and Multilingual Books

One advantage of books with bilingual texts is that the reader need not be fluent in the second language. For instance, Rebecca Emberley's *My Day/Mi día* is an excellent book in English and Spanish that can teach English speakers Spanish words and that can reinforce Spanish-speaking children's first language as well as extend their English-language development. "I wake up in the morning. I brush my teeth and wash my face. I get dressed." "Me levanto en la mañana. Me cepillo los dientes y me lavo la cara. Me visto" (pp. 3–4). The double-page spread of pictures show "toothbrushes/*los cepillos de dientes*," "sink/*el lavabo*," "towel/*la toalla*," and "soap/*el jabón*." The English/Spanish text helps children see and hear words "in action" within English and Spanish syntax. Children also learn similarities and differences in syntax in the two texts: the English "I wake up" starts with the pronoun while the Spanish *"Me levanto"* begins with a reflexive *me*. The individual pictures with English/Spanish labels help children learn new words and vocabulary and provide an excellent one-to-one correspondence of word to object.

Children who are bilingual or English-language learners also benefit from books in two or more languages, but not within the same text. For example, Margaret Wise Brown's *Goodnight Moon* is available in Spanish as *Buenas Noches Luna*. The famous line in English of "In the great green room . . ." becomes "En la enorme habitación verde . . ." in the Spanish translation. In a classic book such as this, where the spare text says so much and the illustrations so beautifully both complement and extend the text, children learn new vocabulary and syntax in two languages through memorizing the memorable text and linking it to the pictures. Even on the first page there is so much to look at and choose in terms of vocabulary. Children learning English can look for the "telephone" and the "red balloon" and any other English words for objects (*lamp, bed, window, stars, rug, table, fire, clock, bears, cow*). Similarly, children learning Spanish can point out and identify *un teléfono* and *un globo rojo* and any other objects that we and they may wish to point out and discover (*cama, ventana, vaca, cepillo, peine, tazón lleno de caldo*). Additional recommended bilingual and multilingual children's books are listed at the end of Chapter 3.

If bilingual or translated books are not readily available in a certain language, or are too expensive, find someone to translate and write in the translation. For example, my daughter, Kaili, who at the time was 3 years old, loved *Goodnight Moon*, but we could not find a version in Tagalog. So her grandmother simply provided one by writing in the Tagalog translation below the existing English text on each page of *Goodnight Moon*. Not only did she provide Kaili with a bilingual text on the spot, but she also allowed Kaili to see her translate the words and syntax from English into Tagalog. "In the great green room" became "Sa malaki at berdeng silid." Kaili's grandmother did the same for Eric Carle's *Have You Seen My Cat?* "Have you seen my cat?" became "Nakita mo ba ang aking pusa?" and "This is not my cat!" became "Hindi ko pusa ito!" A visual advantage of someone simply writing in the translation into another language is that the new text can be written either above or below the original published text. For instance, Kaili's grandmother wrote the Tagalog above the English and also wrote it in larger print. This gave the Tagalog translation a more prominent position (often in published bilingual texts, the English version goes first).

Books with Objects and Props

When I use felt pieces for the animals in Bill Martin and Eric Carle's *Brown Bear, Brown Bear, What Do You See?* both preschoolers and kindergartners enjoy them; the pieces stimulate further engagement with the story. Sometimes I will put out the animals in plain view for the children as I read the book. This is especially helpful for English-language learners who need reinforcement and practice in matching the animal that they see with the animal's name that they hear. I also vary this by giving out a few animals to each child; the children have a chance to display each animal as it is introduced in the book. I further extend this format by putting away the book altogether, and just use the animal felt pieces to tell the story. The children usually remember the order of each animal's entrance into the story, and if they and I don't, we refer back to the book. This kind of retelling of the story using *only* the felt animals is also good practice in sequencing the story. As the children and I retell the story, using the actual language and movement of the book with the animal pieces (and without the book as visual support), the children actively engage in an oral retelling of the story via the felt pieces.

Nonfiction or Informational Books

Nonfiction and informational books, as discussed in Chapter 3, are excellent additions to story books for the read-aloud and informal book-browsing section of the four-part small-group format. Many children are hungry for information and knowledge about their world that only information and content books can provide. In one project, I collected some water from a lake, hoping to find tadpoles. I brought the water sample to a group of preschoolers who wanted to know about tadpoles. I brought in Elizabeth Lacey's *The Complete Frog: A Guide for the Very Young Naturalist*. This is the kind of informative and content-rich resource that provides young children with new words (*naturalist, cold-blooded, amphibian*) and ideas (how to distinguish a toad from a frog) that promote nascent memories for linking the language of science with the science of everyday life.

The Complete Frog is a long book with some complicated text, which I adjust for young children; it is possible to adapt these kinds of informational books without watering down the information and ideas. Young children, even preschoolers, will be interested in their content. The children were fascinated with the characteristics of distinguishing a frog from a toad: the common toad has "thick bumpy skin" and "largish bumps behind the eyes," while the common frog has "soft smooth skin" and "long ridges down each side of the back." Preschooler Leilani found a connection right away: "It's just like Frog and Toad! That's what they look like." (She was referring to the characters from Arnold Lobel's *Frog and Toad Are Friends*). For English-language learners, such informational books are excellent resources for language learning; this book has clear, informative visuals and contains information that grabs children's attention immediately. (Some of the language of the text will need to be simplified and explained.)

Keith DuQuette's *They Call Me Woolly: What Animals Names Can Tell Us* is another informational book that promotes an understanding of the animal world: "Blue-tongued or burrowing, woolly or whooping, there's much to discover in an animal's name. A name can tell you where an animal is from: the African alligator and the American alligator. Or it can tell you about the animal's habitat: the polar bear and the mountain goat" (p. 1). The text is less complicated than *The Complete Frog*, and so there is no need to adapt or change the syntax or vocabulary. The illustrations provide excellent language and literacy support for English-language learners through the clear emphasis on action ("Some animals are named for how they move around: the grasshopper, the burrowing owl and the roadrunner"), sounds ("or the sounds they make with their wings or tails: the hummingbird and the rattlesnake"), and sights ("The zebra butterfly, the leopard frog and the tiger salamander are named for other animals with spots or stripes like theirs"). The animal names can be acted out, listened to, and easily looked at—all helping English-language learners to match sensory experiences with the names for each animal. At the back of the book is a list containing a short paragraph with additional information about each animal, with its picture. One preschooler liked the "horned devil" and the "evil devil" (the Tasmanian devil)—"It's thorny and it has slippers" (that is, its feet look like slippers!). Many informational books have this kind of end-of-book reference section and additions, which provide children with an excellent opportunity to recap and extend the book.

Preschoolers and kindergartners can interact and engage with the alphabet in creative, inventive ways that promote literacy play *and* knowledge of the alphabet. Learning about the alphabet is critical for children's early literacy development—important for reading and for writing—and yet it should not be the sole prerequisite for literacy teaching and learning. All children progress at different rates and in different ways, and the more our literacy philosophies (and how we integrate alphabet-related activities into our teaching) can be tailored to our children's individual, social, cultural, and linguistic needs and talents, the more powerful and long-lasting our collective memories for literacy will be.

A small-group format for children's literacy involvement and growth provides children with close, personal opportunities to interact with the alphabet, words, books, adults, and one another. An established format—such as the one described in this chapter—provides children with an established order and routine for exploring books and working and playing in literacy-related activities. Working in small groups provides time and space for one-to-one interactions, and allows us to focus on observing, understanding, and supporting the linguistic and literacy needs of English-language learners.

Suggested Activities

1. Write down or draw a few of the instant memories you have about learning to read. If you learned to read in a language based on an alphabetic system, what was easy for you? What was hard? What strategies and materials (your own and those of others) were helpful? If you learned to read in a nonalphabetic language system such as Chinese, how might your memories of learning to read inform your philosophy and vision of introducing young children to reading?

2. If you work with English-language learners, make a list of what is challenging and what is easier for them in learning to read in English. Then make another list of ways that you could provide further support for meeting the challenges that you have listed.

3. Draw a web of all the different ways that you structure and organize your groupings of students. Consider how you could add more time, resources, and opportunities for small-group language and literacy teaching and learning. Make a concrete plan for implementing more small-group experiences as a modest beginning change.

4. Consider the small-group language and literacy format and components presented and discussed in this chapter. What elements of the format do you find most valuable, and which components would you most like to implement?

5. Examine the range of books and reading resources that you have in your classroom. Do children have access to all these materials? Is there a good mix of children's literature and content or informational books? If not, collect additional content and informational books that offer several ways that the books can be introduced and used by the children.

USEFUL RESOURCES

Alphabet Knowledge and Early Reading Development

Adams, M. J. (1990). *Beginning to read: Thinking and learning about print*. Cambridge, MA: MIT Press.

Bussis, A., Chittenden, E., Amarel, M., & Klausner, E. (1985). *Inquiry into meaning*. Hillsdale, NJ: Earlbaum.

Clay, M. (1998). *By different paths to common outcomes*. York, ME: Stenhouse.

Clay, M. (2001). *Change over time in children's literacy development*. Auckland, NZ: Heinemann.

Dragon, P. B. (2001). *Literacy from day one*. Portsmouth, NH: Heinemann.

Ferreiro, E., & Teberosky, A. (1982). *Literacy before schooling*. Exeter, NH: Heinemann.

Hiebert, E. H., & Taylor, B. M. (Eds.). (1995). *Getting reading right from the start: Effective early literacy interventions*. Boston: Allyn & Bacon.

Holdaway, D. (1979). *Foundations of literacy*. New York: Ashton Scholastic.

Houle, A., & Krogress, A. (2001). The wonders of word walls. *Young Children, 56*(5), 92–95.

Meier, D. R. (2000). *Scribble scrabble: Learning to read and write with diverse teachers, children, and families*. New York: Teachers College Press.

Neuman, S. B., & Dickinson, D. K. (Eds.). (2001). *The handbook of early literacy research*. New York: Guilford Press.

Owocki, G. (1999). *Literacy through play*. Portsmouth, NH: Heinemann.

Roskos, K. A., Christie J. F., & Richgels, D. J. (2003). The essentials of early literacy instruction. *Young Children, 58*(2), 52–60.

Snow, C. E., Burns, S., & Griffin, P. (1998). *Preventing reading difficulties in young children*. Washington, DC: National Academy Press.

Spodek, B., & Saracho, O. N. (Eds.). (1993). *Language and literacy in early childhood education: Yearbook in early childhood education* (Vol. 4). New York: Teachers College Press.

Teale, W., & Sulzby, E. (Eds.) (1986). *Emergent literacy: Writing and reading*. Norwood, NJ: Ablex.

Children's Books Cited in Chapter 4

Brown, M. W. (1939). *The noisy book*. New York: Harper & Row.

Brown, M. W. (1947). *Goodnight moon*. New York: HarperCollins.

Brown, M. W. (1995). *Buenas noches luna*. Mexico City, Mexico: Sistemas Técnicos de Edición.

Bryan, A. (1997). *Ashley Bryan's abc of African American poetry*. New York: Atheneum.

Carle, E. (1987). *Have you seen my cat?* New York: Simon & Schuster.

Cummings, P. (1998). *My aunt came back*. New York: HarperCollins.

DuQuette, K. (2002). *They call me woolly: What animal names can tell us*. New York: G. P. Putnam's Sons.

Ehlert, L. (1989). *Eating the alphabet: Fruits and vegetables from a to z*. San Diego: Harcourt Brace.

Emberley, R. (1993). *My day/Mi día*. Boston: Little Brown.

Hague, M. (1993). *Teddy bear, teddy bear*. New York: William & Morrow.

Lacey, E. (1989). *The complete frog: A guide for the very young naturalist*. New York: Lothrop, Lee & Shepard Books.

Lobel, A. (1970). *Frog and Toad are friends*. New York: HarperCollins.

Martin, B., & Carle, E. (1967). *Brown bear, brown bear, What do you see?* New York: Holt, Rinehart & Winston.

Martin, B., & Carle, E. (1991). *Polar bear, polar bear, What do you hear?* New York: Henry Holt.

Oxenbury, H. (1987). *Tickle, tickle*. New York: Simon & Schuster.

Pinkney, A., & Pinkney, B. (1997). *Shake, shake, shake*. San Diego, CA: Red Wagon Books.

Shannon, G. (1996). *Tomorrow's alphabet*. New York: Mulberry Books.

Additional Recommended Alphabet Books

Aagard, J. (1989). *The calypso alphabet*. New York: Henry Holt.

Bourke, L. (1991). *Eye spy: A mysterious alphabet*. San Francisco: Chronicle.

Brown, R. (1991). *Alphabet times four: An international abc*. New York: Dutton.

Bryan, A. (1997). *Ashley Bryan's abc of African American poetry*. New York: Athaneum.

Cline-Ransom, L. (2001). *Quilt alphabet*. New York: Holiday House.

Fain, K. (1993). *Handsigns: A sign language alphabet*. San Francisco: Chronicle.

Hoban, T. (1995). *26 letters and 99 cents*. New York: Harper Trophy.

Nathan, C. (1995). *Bugs and beasties abc*. Boca Rotan, FL: Cool Kids Press.

Rosario, I. (1981). *Project abc/Proyecto abc: An urban alphabet book in English and Spanish*. New York: Holt.

Rotner, S. (1996). *Action alphabet*. New York: Atheneum Books.

Ryden, H. (1989). *Wild animals of Africa abc*. New York: Lode Star Books.

Shannon, G. (1996). *Tomorrow's alphabet*. New York: Greenwillow Books.

Shaw, E. (1997). *Grandmother's alphabet: Grandma can be anything from a to z*. Duluth, MN: Pfeifer-Hamilton.

Wells, R. (1992). *A to zen*. New York: Simon and Schuster.

Yorinko, A. (1999). *The alphabet atlas*. New York: Winslow.

Young, E. (1997). *Voices of the heart*. New York: Scholastic.

Chapter 5

Drawing, Writing, and Dictation

der carul and lwes i wil mis you a lot i hop that you hav a godsorigvakshn irile liked sgol and I wil nkstyer bi [Dear Carol and Louise, I will miss you a lot. I hope that you have a good summer vacation. I really liked school and I will next year. Bye.]

—Noah, a kindergartner, writing an end-of-the-year note to his two teachers, Carol and Louise

TEACHING AND LEARNING QUESTIONS

1. How can writing promote a sense of classroom community? How can we make children's writing activities developmentally and culturally responsive?
2. How do children integrate writing and drawing?
3. What do young children's early writings reveal about their understanding of sound-symbol relationships and writing as a symbol system?
4. What is dictation and what are effective strategies for using dictation to promote children's understanding of reading and writing?
5. How can we support the early writing of English-language learners? What are helpful strategies and what strategies do the children themselves use?

WRITING AS COMMUNITY-BUILDING

We write in order to express ourselves, make connections with others, and better understand the worlds we live in, both real and imagined. We also write to record, preserve, and revisit our memories of our childhoods and our current lives. Learning to write, and learning to write well, starts with the vision of children as engaged and excited about the mechanics of writing (handwriting, spelling, punctuation, sound-symbol relationships) and the creative, artistic side of writing (expressing imaginations, hopes, dreams, failures, and disappointments; drawing on varied literary forms and traditions; interweaving Englishes and other languages). We must keep both goals in mind (i.e., 1. the mechanical, and 2. the artistic), for it is so easy for us (especially in the current climate of giving attention to literacy as a mechanical process and not an art) to focus solely or almost entirely on the mechanics of learning to write.

An excellent way to meld the two is to embed writing within the social fabric of the classroom. For example, in Chapter 1, I discussed how Kaitlin, a kindergarten teacher, had her class interview the school's farm and gardening teacher, Rachel. The interview provided the children with a language-and-literacy experience in which they became the expert users of language through interviewing an adult. Kaitlin used a large visual of a web to frame the children's questions and Rachel's answers. Kaitlin wrote "Rachel" in the center of the web and then webbed out the children's individual questions in preparation for the interview (see Figure 5.1). The web is also excellent support for English-language learners, who can use the visual to help them understand the form and function of the interviews. During the interview, Kaitlin jotted down Rachel's responses to each question as the children asked Rachel their questions.

JOSEPH: Do you like teaching kids?
RACHEL: I love teaching kids! And teaching you where your food comes from. You also teach me.

Later, Kaitlin typed up the children's questions and Rachel's responses in a standard interview format for the children to see and refer to. Kaitlin repeated this activity by inviting the school's two farm and gardening volunteers, Sarah and Joe, to be interviewed by the children. By this time, the children were familiar with asking questions about the teachers and about the garden.

Figure 5.1. Preparatory Web for Interviewing Rachel

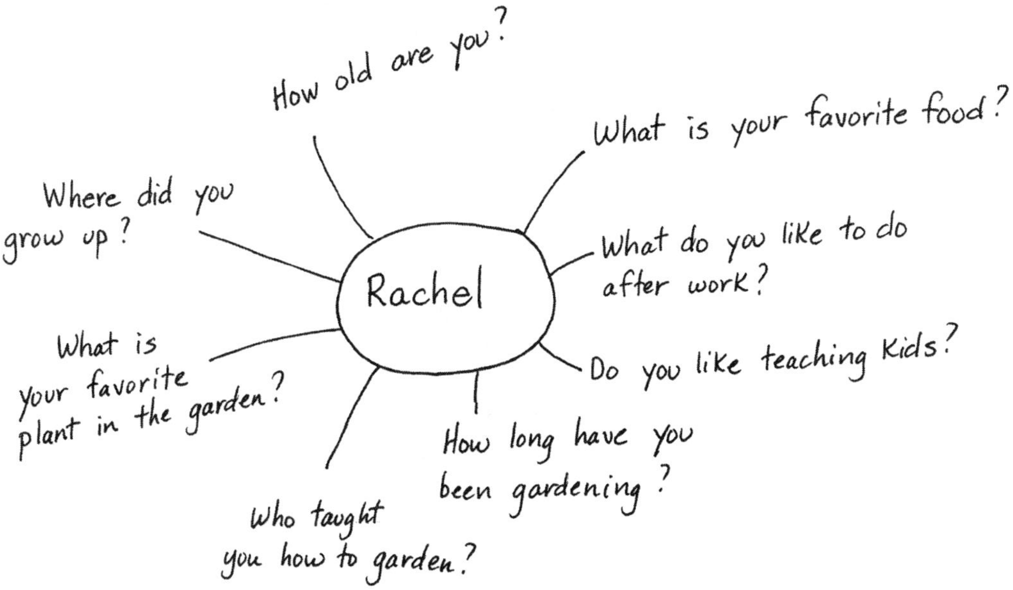

ARTISHA: How long have you been gardening?
SARAH: Since I was a little girl. And my mom has been gardening since
she was little and her mom has been gardening since she was a
little girl. The women in my family have always gardened. And
now I'm teaching my daughter how to garden.

For Joe's interview, Kaitlin drew a big chicken on the paper with Joe's name
inside (he helped with the chickens in the farm and garden), and then
webbed out the children's questions and Joe's responses.

DONALD: Does chicken pox come from chickens?
JOE: No. Chicken pox actually comes from cows. It's cowpox.
ASIA: How do the chickens sleep?
JOE: They sleep in a coop, so raccoons won't eat them. The coop is up
high so they can roost up high. They line up on a bar.
KAI: Where did you get the chickens?
JOE: I got them from Big Pet Shop in our city. Chickens from pet stores
have shots. I get them as chicks.

The interviews allowed the children to learn more about both their gardening teachers and the animals and plants in their school garden. By actively
taking charge of the interviewing, and in seeing how oral language (their
questions) and written language (the webbed written questions and answers
and the final typed-up interview) connect, the children learned to see how
they could use writing to learn about the immediate social world at school.
    In another example of writing that promotes social cohesion and
community-building, Kaitlin asked the children to draw, write, or dictate
content about how they help one another in the classroom. This is an excellent activity both for the beginning of the school year, to let children know
that this is something to be valued for the year, and for later in the year as
a reminder to children of how far they have come as members of an intellectual and social community.

JACQUELINE: I helped Maya because she was crying. I said she can play
with me.
NYELEY: Maria hurt her face. I helped her up.
JOSEPH: The bees were stinging Eric, and I helped chase them away.
Actually it was Marcos!
ANGEL: I'm taking care of Hiroshi when we're outside playing in the
grass. He fell off the gate. I helped him. He fell in the pool and
there were ants in them.
RIO: Julia is crying. She was bleeding because she fell down and the ball
hit her when she was playing soccer. I put out my hand to pick her
up. She was too heavy so I held her hand. That helped her feel
better.

Since accidents are always a big draw with young children, this kind of activity perfectly melds children's fascination with accidents and the recounting of situations when they assist their classmates. When these kinds of writing activities are multiplied many times over in a classroom, they help children see how writing can strengthen the social fabric of the classroom community.

PERSONAL JOURNALS

Key Components and Ideas

As I explained in Chapter 4, in the third phase of the small-group literacy format that I use with preschoolers and kindergartners, I have the children make their own personal journals, in which they can draw or write. These journals promote a social sense of the power of writing, drawing, and dictation. There are several key components for the effective design and use of these journals.

Materials and Organization

I use recycled paper (all blank with no lines) and staple about 12 pages between an 11" × 17" piece of colorful construction paper. I ask each child to write his or her name on the front of their journal and to decorate the cover with magazine pictures. As children finish their journals, I hold on to them so that I can show the children and their families the children's ongoing writing development—interests/content, alphabet knowledge, syntax, English vocabulary, and sharing and collaboration with other children. I then ask each child to number each new journal for easy chronological tracking. Each time we do our personal journals, I review some of the journals and point out what certain children have been doing, and I ask the children if they want to continue their recent drawing or writing or would prefer to do something different. Some children regularly like to revisit and add on to a previous journal entry, while others are eager to keep going and do a new page.

Content

The small-group format allows time and space for the children and me to talk and think about what they may draw and write. Although I do not ask the children to write and draw about particular topics in their journals (though I do ask in other kinds of writing activities), I rarely find a child who cannot think of a topic. If a child does become stuck, I often ask him or her to look back over previous journal entries, use some of our books or other literacy materials as a springboard, or talk with a friend and find out what he or she is doing in his or her journal. For instance, some children like to choose the name cards for their class and copy all the names on their journal page. Others like to take one of our read-aloud books and copy the text and illustrations; this is especially helpful for English-language learners, as they can see and manipulate whole words and sentences in English.

I have found that children most often write and draw about the following content:

> Family and friends
> Classmates and school
> Popular culture and media (television, movies, toys)
> Games, sports, and playing
> Cars and trucks
> Nature and the outdoors
> The city and urban areas
> Colors, letters, numbers
> Books and stories

Children follow their individual interests and most often choose just a few of these content areas to pursue over the course of the year.

Drawing and Writing: Using Symbols

Opportunities to draw, use art, and write in an integrated way allows children to experiment and play with their developing understanding of drawing and writing as symbol systems. For example, as shown in Plate 1, preschooler Leilani creates an array of figures, numerals, and letters all on the same page.

By combining drawn (sun, faces, objects, designs) and written (letters and numbers) symbols, Leilani experiments with drawing and writing as complementary symbol systems. It makes sense, to a 3½-year-old, to combine a drawing of a sun and letters and numbers on the very same page. From Leilani's perspective, all her markings are equally powerful and meaningful as symbols—drawing and writing allow Leilani to place these objects and designs one step away from her. They move from her mind and heart to her hand and then to the paper, making a "literal and symbolic leap" from her internal thoughts and feelings to the external world of the written and drawn page.

Understanding this kind of transformation is critical for promoting young children's intrinsic motivation for playing with symbols through drawing and writing. Pursuing this combination of drawing and writing, Leilani, as a fast-developing three-year-old, gains important experiences in discovering what is pleasing to the hand and eye—to her senses. In this way, what she creates—something borrowed from previous drawing and writ-

ing experiences (such as letters or numbers or a picture of the sun) or something created right on the spot (such as the designs in the middle of her
picture)—constitute early developmental artistic exploration. As an artist,
Leilani *engages herself* or self-scaffolds the process of selecting shapes,
colors, contours, depth, foregrounding, movement, and other aspects of
rendering her inner world in a representative, symbolic way. This is a
powerful process that complements what Leilani and other children might
do in reading, whereby they take and interpret books and texts, for in
drawing and writing Leilani produces and creates the text, images, and
symbols. In effect, she is creating her own memories for literacy and drawing from scratch.

In Plate 2, Sarina, a 5-year-old kindergartner, reveals a similar process
for a slightly older child. Sarina saw a picture of SpongeBob Squarepants, a
television character, drawn by another child and wanted to draw her own.
(Unfamiliar with this popular television character, I incorrectly interpreted
her label for her drawing as Spongeball.) Like Leilani, Sarina knows that
she can depict objects and characters and write numerals and letters all on
the same page—it makes fine developmental sense to her. And like Leilani,
Sarina experiments with drawn and written symbols to create an overall
artistic effect of shape, color, contour, direction and movement, and meaning. A little further along developmentally than Leilani in terms of writing
conventions (spelling, letter formation, handwriting), Sarina experiments
with writing strings of letters across her page and in and around her drawn
figures and designs.

Although I was aware that Sarina knew most of her letters and
sounds, and therefore could begin matching letters with certain sounds to
spell at least parts of words, I supported her interest in writing sentence-
like strings of random letters. This is another example of self-scaffolding in
which Sarina experiments with forming letters of her choice in an artistic
and spontaneous way. In this way, she ensures herself total control over
the artistic experience with her drawing and writing. Any insistence from
me that she only write in collaboration with me, as I helped her spell all
words correctly, would have taken a good measure of the direction and control of her writing and drawing away from her. After Sarina drew and wrote,
we did do the dictation together. Sarina pointed to the wordlike and sentence-
like strings of letters, and using her finger to slide along the string, "translated" each one for me. I wrote down *Granny* for her written *kimmir* in the
bottom right-hand corner of her page. She dictated what I thought was
Spongeball and *Patrick* for two of the figures in the middle of her drawing. In
the span of 15 minutes, Sarina accomplished a great deal. She worked on
dual symbolic levels (drawing characters/figures and writing numerals/
letters/words); wrote, drew, dictated, and conversed; integrated her out-
of-school interest in SpongeBob and her family into her school journal; and
worked independently and in collaboration with me.

Drawing, Writing, and Social Interaction

Children who are writing, drawing, and dictating in their journals often literally and figuratively draw in their peers. Preschoolers Juan and Donna help each other as they draw in their journals.

JUAN: Make yours smell pretty! [i.e., by using a scented magic marker]. Give me your marker. (Juan draws the same shape on Donna's page for her on his journal page.) Here, I made you a dinosaur. It's cool. So be cool.
DONNA: Make me a man now here. (Juan draws in Donna's journal)
JUAN: I made you a man, but I made you a vampire!

The drawing allows Juan, an English-language learner, to use his drawing talents and affinity for kid lingo in English ("It's cool. So be cool") to interact and converse with Donna. In this way, Juan's drawing (which requires no oral language in English) facilitates social interaction and conversation with Donna.

Some children like Aaron make a game-like opening for others to pay attention to their drawing:

You don't know what I'm making [i.e. drawing], Shakira. Look at my paper. (A few moments later . . .) I'm going to make a door because my momma likes it when I make a pink door.

Other children, such as Latrina, like to inform their peers what is permissible to draw: "I'm making mine's pretty. You can do anything with your paper like good or bad." Some children use conversational language that they know will grab the attention of their peers (at least for a moment). Alexis emphasizes, "Y'all better like mine—mine's gonna be hecka good." Other children entice their peers in *as* they draw and create their characters and objects. Craig explains, "Here go my alligator. Here go my leg. My leg is messed up. Now I need to make a rainbow!"

In order to promote a sense of anticipation for the group of children, I sometimes ask them, *before* they draw and write, what they will do. As each child speaks, the other children usually listen in and spontaneously make their own contributions.

MARQUEZ: I'm going to make a face. I'm going to make my daddy and my bike.
JEMIMA: I'm going to make an apple and trees and a boy and a girl and books.
ARTHUR: I'm going to make a tree and a lion and a koala bear and a bear.

This thinking and sharing out loud is a form of making memories for literacy before children actually draw and write. It adds an element of suspense and anticipation—will their drawings and writing really turn out the way the children predicted?—and thus adds to a sense of a community of young writers and artists.

Supporting English-Language Learners

Copying, Collaborating, and Scaffolding

English-language learners, especially in early stages of learning English, need opportunities for reproducing drawings and writing done by peers as well as those found in books and other literacy sources. In their early literacy learning, English-language learners rely on using basic linguistic knowledge in a new language. Copying is an effective self-scaffolding strategy for these learners because they do not need to use oral or written language—they can just look at and reproduce what they see.

Most often, English-language learners copy from English-language materials that are readily accessible and that provide clues for recognizing and understanding patterns in the unfamiliar new language. When a first language has a script that looks different from that of English (Hebrew, Farsi, Arabic, Chinese, and Hindi are just a few examples), personal journal writing encourages English-language learners to gain experience in forming, recognizing, and experiencing letters and words in English. For example, Huma, an Urdu-speaking kindergartner from Pakistan, loved to write all the letters of the alphabet time after time. She took the plastic letters, arranged them from A-to-Z, and then transferred them in A-to-Z order onto her journal page.

Huma also loved to copy the name cards from her class. She would turn to me and say, "Names?" And I knew what she meant. Huma knew that her simple one-word question would do the trick. Huma sat with the whole pile of name cards, carefully turning them over one at a time and writing each name on her journal page until she had finished the entire class. This is an example of self-scaffolding by an English-language learner because Huma (1) is revisiting the name cards that we use in the opening part of our small group format, (2) is using small chunks (children's names) of language in English that she hears all day long in her classroom, and (3) can refer these language chunks in a one-to-one correspondence to the actual children in the room.

Huma often held up a name card for me to read to be sure of the name before she wrote it down. This required no oral English on her part, only her holding up the card to get my attention. She was also concerned about learning how to read each name card. Huma delighted in finding a name card from someone in our immediate small group, and would show the card to that person. Thus, the name cards can help English-language learners initiate social contact with peers without dependence on oral language and correct English vocabulary and syntax.

Ismele, a newly arrived kindergartner from Mexico, was also in the early stages of learning English. Like Huma, her classmate, she also liked to write down all the children's names from their class. Ismele and Huma loved to sit side by side with the pile of name cards, each writing a name down and then handing that card to the other person. One day in early February, for instance, Ismele wrote down all the class names one after the other in seven neat rows. By the end, she had filled in her entire journal page for a total of 20 names and more than 80 letters in English. At the end of her journal, I helped her dictate and write, "I like the names," which she wrote in at the bottom of the page. Two days later, Ismele wrote the names again, and this time she wrote groups of names in different colors of magic markers: black, bright yellow, and bright pink.

On one occasion, Ismele and Huma were working side by side on their journals. They spoke only a little English (their common language) as they drew, but watched each other draw. Ismele drew an outdoor scene in vivid colors. Huma, a less accomplished artist, drew several shapes, less easily recognizable. After finishing, Ismele dictated first, pointed to an object, and said, "Sun, clouds, flower, tree" in one-word labels for each object. Huma, listening and watching Ismele, pointed to her drawn objects one by one and dictated, "Bubble gum, tree, tree, house, cake." I do not know if Huma had originally intended to draw something resembling trees, but Ismele's work most likely influenced Huma to also include trees in her drawing and dictation. Possibly, too, she wanted to differentiate herself from Ismele by dictating "cake, bubble gum, and house." In this way, Huma and Ismele's collaboration in their drawing (without oral language in English) influenced their English-language content (words that relate such as *tree* and *flower*) and structure (nouns, both singular and plural). Further, Ismele's dictation influenced Huma's, as Huma both borrowed from and then differentiated herself from Ismele's dictation.

English-Language Learners and Native Speakers of Varied Englishes

The small-group format can facilitate social, language, and literacy collaboration between English-language learners and native speakers of varied Englishes. These are often instances of peer-to-peer language and literacy scaffolding in which children themselves further one another's learning in developmentally and culturally responsive ways. On one occasion, kindergartners Lupe (an English-language learner) and Paris (an African American child speaking Standard English and African American English) worked side by side on their journals. During our few previous small-group times, Lupe and Paris had loved to read a book about a cat and a dog. Plates 3 and 4 show their journal entries as Lupe and Paris collaborated on their writing, drawing, and dictation.

Lupe and Paris' collaboration paralleled the book's story line and illustrations. In the book, the cat and dog both do the same things, one after the other—the cat takes out paints and so does the dog, the cat draws a flower and then the dog does, and so on. This imitation and I'll-do-what-you-do from the book appealed—socially, intellectually, and culturally—to Paris and Lupe and promoted their own I'll-do-what-you-do in their journals.

As in the other examples of young children's drawing and writing, Lupe and Paris want to pack a variety of symbols into a single journal entry. Lupe started to write the phrases "the diser," "the biser," "the biser" at the top delighting in the silliness of these words. Paris thought it funny, too. This got the two children off to a good social start as they worked side by side—it became the glue for their collaboration. Lupe then copied "the dog took out the paints" from the book, writing the words vertically on the right side of her journal page. At this time, Paris copied down "cat and dog" from the book, writing it in the middle of her page. The two children then both drew their rendering of the painting easel pictured in the book, both carefully and closely drawing the same picture in their separate journals. They were both quite pleased with themselves and with each other. For their dictation, they both chose, "The dog is here." This kind of synchrony between written, copied, drawn, and dictated texts builds social and intellectual bridges between English-language learners and speakers of varied Englishes.

Drawing, Art, and Writing

English-language learners often rely on art for rendering in a representational and symbolic manner their experiences, objects, feelings, and thoughts. As makes good language-learning sense, English-language learners most often start with what they already know in English. Here are some examples:

- Suri, a preschooler newly arrived from India, liked to draw small lines in different-colored magic markers, and for her dictation with me she'd point to and identify each color—"red, red, pink, yellow, green, red"—for each mark made in her journal page.
- For several weeks, Julia, another preschooler, also relied on her knowledge of color names in English when working in her journal. On February 7, Julia drew large patches in several different colors and dictated (as she pointed to the colors) the following about her drawing to me, "I know my colors! Purple, green, red, brown, blue, orange." On February 21, she wrote her name and

rows of random numbers, letters, and squiggles. As she pointed to each part of her drawing, Julia dictated to me, "I like pink. More pink. Orange. Red. Orange. Red. Red. Red." On March 13, Julia wrote several columns of letters, and pointing to each column, dictated to me, "Orange. Orange. Orange. Purple. Pink."

- Luis, a kindergartner, loved to draw tic-tac-toe grids in his journal over several weeks. He was fascinated with the game, and drew grid after grid and engaged his classmates and me in playing tic-tac-toe with him. Luis, who needed support in his handwriting, also practiced copying and writing "tic-tac-toe" for several weeks. So while I encouraged Luis to draw his favorite game, I also encouraged him to work on his letter formation so he could do some writing on his own.

Popular Culture as a Springboard

As Plate 5 shows, Isabel, a Spanish-speaking kindergartner with some familiarity with English, loved to draw the Powerpuff Girls, who are popular on television and in books. The flowing, floating Powerpuff Girls rise up and move out of her journal page, engaging not only Isabel but also her classmates seated nearby. They want Isabel to draw and help them draw Powerpuff figures in their journals, which Isabel willingly does, and I encourage this kind of interaction with both her Spanish-speaking and English-speaking classmates. Talking and sharing her drawings provide Isabel with extended opportunities to converse in Spanish and to extend her English-language development based on her nonverbal drawing.

Over the course of several weeks during the middle of her kindergarten year, Isabel liked to draw and dictate the Powerpuff Girls' names (Buttercup, Blossom, and Bubbles) and other text for her Powerpuff Girl creations. In her early writing of the names, Isabel identified each Girl for me, and I alternated between writing down the name for her and telling Isabel how to spell selected aspects of the Girls' names, which she wrote down. As she pointed to the Girl on the right, Isabel said, "Bubbles," and I wrote it above and to the right of the figure. She then identified "Buttercup," and I gave the sounds for *b, t,* and *c* and Isabel correctly supplied the corresponding letters that make these sounds. When I wrote these letters, I underlined each of them to show Isabel which letters she knew. (This strategy also helped remind me later which letter-sound correspondences Isabel could identify at the time.) Since Isabel knew how to write a majority of the letters in English, I told her all the letters to write *Blossom,* which she did twice in the middle of the page. Later on, in other journal entries, I encouraged Isabel to look back at previous journal pages such as that shown in Plate 5, so she could copy the names and words without my assistance. This encouraged self-scaffolding on Isabel's part.

EFFECTIVE DICTATION STRATEGIES

Dictation, or the writing down of oral language, is a key tool for promoting children's early writing development. It encourages children to use their considerable oral language talents and connects to their drawing and art. Since dictation is carried out with another person, it provides excellent support for English-language learners, who benefit from close interaction with an adult or another child. There are several effective dictation strategies that promote various aspects of children's early literacy development.

Link Drawing, Dictation, and Writing

Dictation encourages one-to-one interaction between adults and children and helps young children build their knowledge of connections between oral and written language. Plate 6 shows how Emile, an African American kindergartner, linked drawing, writing, and dictation all on one page. Emile chose to work on this one journal entry twice, first in early January and then again in early February. On the first occasion, Emile drew his "25 car," complete with wheels, steering column, and red exhaust and fire coming out of the back. He worked carefully to depict each part of the car and talked about it with excitement and engagement. He dictated a simple statement, "This is my 25 car," which I wrote down. Then he wanted to write *car* and *me*, and so I wrote these for him at the top of the page and added small boxes underneath. Emile, who needed some extra support in his letter formation and writing, benefited from having the small boxes for writing in the letters for the words.

Emile returned to the "25 car" entry one month later. He added a little more detail to the drawing and more dictation. He told me that a "friend" was in the middle of the car, another "person" was in the back, and he was in the front "pushing the button" to make the car move. Instead of writing this for him, I asked him to help me spell certain words (*the*) and identify selected letters to represent certain sounds that I provided for him (*b* and *t* and *n* in *button*, *p* and *r* and *s* and *n* in *person*, *f* and *n* in *friend*). By concentrating on these consonants and letter-sound correspondences that I felt he would know at this point, Emile and I scaffolded the dictation-writing together, providing both of us with evidence and the experience of identifying the correct sound-symbol correspondences. He was pleased!

Make It Social

Dictation works well when children are engaged with adults and other children and when there is a strong social reason and "push" behind the dictation. For example, writing on a large piece of chart paper, Kaitlin asked her kindergarten class on the first day of school, "How do you feel today?" During a whole-class activity on the rug, each child contributed one sentence, and Kaitlin wrote his or her name at the end. To start off, she and the student teacher, Gopal, gave their answers.

> I feel excited. *Kaitlin*
> I feel a little bit nervous. *Gopal*
> I feel really happy. *Julia (English-language learner)*
> I feel good. *Kelly*
> I feel happy. *Antawn*
> I feel happy. *Shanika*
> I feel happy. *Raul (English-language learner)*
> I feel nervous. *Marjorie*
> I feel happy. *Anita*
> I feel happy. *Arthur*
> I feel happy. *Marika*

The English syntax and sentence length that Kaitlin and Gopal model are simple and easily understood by all the children. This provides excellent support for English-language learners. For example, since Julia, an English-language learner, follows the two sentences by the teachers, she has two example sentences (and forms of English syntactical structure) to follow and use if she wishes. As it turns out, she uses the first two words and adds two different words of her own. In general, the repetitive and consistent structure of the sentences beginning with the phrase, "I feel _____" help all the children. They don't have to consider many different possible sentence forms because they can fill in a word or phrase after the initial "I feel _____."

In another example of dictation promoting social cohesion, I worked with a group of preschoolers on taking their dictation via the computer. Since I can type so much faster than I can write, it is often useful for me to use the computer or a typewriter to take children's dictation. Not only does it speed up the process, but they often produce longer pieces of text, it can be easier to "read" back, and young children delight in seeing their dictation immediately printed out. On this occasion, I worked with Anthony while the rest of the children were doing their journals. Just as we were starting, on the spur of the moment, Anthony decided to include his friend Jasmine, who was sitting at the next table with her journal. As soon as he looked over at her, and said her name, to be included in his dictated story, Jasmine looked up and came over to us with a smile.

> Once upon a time there was two kids named Anthony and
> Jasmine. And we lived in a house with no momma and no
> dad. Then we went to find some food in the deep deep
> woods. Then me and Jasmine went to find some plums.
> Some were clean and then we ate them. Then we made a
> house. Then along came Mr. Bad Wolf, and guess what? I

had a straw house and Jasmine had a brick house. The big
bad wolf started with Jasmine's house and then Jasmine ran
to my house, and I closed the door and the wolf huffed and
puffed and he tried to blow my house down but he couldn't
because it was real strong.

By literally dictating her into his story, Anthony uses the dictation activity
to strengthen his friendship with Jasmine.

Connect with Content Knowledge

Since most young children can express themselves and show what
they understand more powerfully through oral language, dictation is an
excellent way for children to further their content or academic knowledge
across the curriculum. In one instance, the children and teachers at a preschool were learning about fish and the ocean. The children read books
about fish, drew pictures, and dictated stories about and reflected on marine life. Here is 4-year-old Leilani's dictation:

The red fish lives in the sea and there is a lot of plants to eat
and there is treasure in the water and there is dolphins
living in the sea, too. She is a friend of the dolphin. The
dolphin has a sister. They like to play together. The red fish
comes over to the dolphin's house to play and sometimes
they have a sleepover. There is a mermaid that guards the
treasure. There is other fishies living in the water, too.

Leilani uses dictation to show part of her emerging knowledge about fish
and marine life and takes advantage of dictation and her oral language
powers to make a "reflective" narrative about what she is learning. She is
beginning to use dictation as a vehicle for a narrative interpretation of what
she is studying.

In another example, when a kindergarten classroom celebrated International Women's Day, the children created artistic renditions of women
they admired and then dictated a text to the teacher about the women they
chose. It made for a colorful and impressive display of women of varied
ages, language and ethnic backgrounds, and familial and friendship relationships. Armani chose to depict her grandmother and to dictate why she
admired and liked her. Armani cut out, glued, and drew a colorful depic-
tion of her grandmother and dictated the following:

My grandma likes kids, art and decorations. She likes me.
She likes everything in the whole wide world. She doesn't
like it when my mommy gets mad at me. She takes me a lot
of places. She takes me to picnics, school and on field trips

> every day. My grandma takes me to a birthday party with a
> lot of crazy boys and a lot of crazy girls. She likes to cook me
> food. My favorite food is spaghetti and fish. She likes carrots
> and takes me to the movies. I love my grandma and she
> loves me. She is my friend.

Armani's teacher placed the dictation and the portrait on the wall with those of the other women whom the children admired.

In another example of linking dictation and children's knowledge, the kindergarten teacher Kaitlin used creative, artistic activities to promote early alphabetic knowledge. The children selected an animal, and also the corresponding letter that started that animal's name, and then drew, cut out (with the teacher's help), and painted and decorated their animal. The children then dictated a text to accompany their animal, and once all the animals were completed, they were put on display to form an exhibit titled "Animals on Parade." Each animal was cut from a double piece of thick tagboard so it could be pulled apart and made to stand upright on its own four, or two, legs. Dictation played a key role in creating the text to accompany each animal. The dictation allowed the children to extend the content of their alphabet learning, and so the activity was not simply a "low-level" matching of objects to their corresponding letters, but a sophisticated mixture of the alphabet, art, animals, dictated text, and a whole-class art exhibit. For example, in "E for Elephant," Susan dictated a large paragraph about the Asian elephant.

> My elephant is an Asian elephant because it has little ears on
> its head and a hump. Elephants' backs are lumpy. Elephants
> eat bark from trees and sometimes roots. Their enemies are
> hyenas and lions. When a baby is first born and the grown-
> up elephants crowd around it to protect it and sometimes a
> young elephant will charge the lions and hyenas to scare
> them away while the grown-ups protect the baby.

Susan and the other children in the class learned information about their animals from books and other reference materials both in the classroom and at home.

Take It on the Road

As mentioned in Chapter 3, the preschool educator Bev Bos advocates the use of in-the-moment dictation with young children. In this strategy, teachers hold clipboards or pieces of paper on which they can take down children's dictations as they approach a teacher. The advantages are several:

- The strategy does not restrict teachers and children to doing dictation at a particular time or place in the classroom, and so it can happen inside or outside the classroom, widening the possible experiences and sights that children might produce dictation about.
- As young children can often not wait if a story or idea pops into their heads, the "instant" dictation opportunity quickly gets their language onto paper to preserve what they want to express.
- The strategy enables children to have quality one-to-one interactions with adults around language and literacy.
- It can be done privately, as some children do not like their ideas and stories to be overhead by other children.
- It's low-tech and easily doable logistically by teachers, requiring only a pen in the pocket and a clipboard.
- It is a routine that children essentially control, since they, rather than adults, are the ones taking the initiative to do the dictation.

Dictation can also literally go home into children's out-of-school lives. At one preschool, the teachers put a small stuffed cat and dog into two separate baskets and each child in turn is given these, along with a small blank book. The children take the animals home and dictate and draw about their adventures with the animals. Once the materials are back at school, the teachers or families (if they are present at morning circle time) read the dictated texts and show the pictures of the children's experiences with the animals. The children love the animals, carrying them with them wherever they go until they return to school. The animals do not have designated names, which allows the children to invent their own names. When the dictated texts are read back to the children at morning circle, the children love to hear each new name given to the animals by the other children. It holds a special fascination for them that the animal can stay the same and yet be called by different names.

The sharing of the dictations and drawings also allow the families at morning circle to learn more about one another's home lives and to hear how other children and adults rendered their experiences with the animals.

Larry: We've [i.e., the cat and I have] been together for a long time. We had a lot of fun together playing chess and checkers. I won! Harold [that's his name] waited in his basket on the floor while I ate dinner. Later we went out into the woods where we saw a wolf. The wolf chased us and bit off Harold's ear. We ran home and went inside to sew Harold's ear back on. We heard a scratching sound but we didn't open the door. We locked it so the wolf couldn't get in. The End

(Larry concluded his entry with a drawing of his house)

Tiffany: Once upon a time there was a kitty in our house in the backyard. She had babies and the babies went to sleep. The mama cat put the babies to sleep. When they woke up they had kitty cat food for breakfast and went to school. The mommy kitty picked them up and they watched t.v. and went to sleep again. They woke up and went to school but they didn't want to but the mommy had to take them to school and then they liked it. They played and danced and danced with me. And then singed and danced and played dress up and then they went back to sleep again and then they went back to their home. The End.

P.S. Rosie ate all the desserts . . . She has a tummy ache.

(Tiffany concluded her entry with a drawing of "Rosie" the kitty)

Farhad: I took the kitty home. It's nice and fresh at home. He's very cute at home and he slept before night. The dog slept in the garden before night too. His face is nice and warm at home. Good bye.

(Farhad concluded his entry by drawing lots of circles on a blank page and then adding some more circles right over his dictation)

For families where the adults are not able to write down children's dictations, the children can still draw the pictures. For families who speak languages other than English, the dictated text can be done in their first language.

Promote Bilingualism/Biliteracy

If children have access to adults or other children who can translate and write in a language other than English, dictation can be used to promote bilingualism and biliteracy. On many occasions, even if we can only offer a few words or phrases in another language for a child, we can still give children the message that we value and want to promote their multilingualism. Lucretia, a preschooler, liked to dictate texts for her journal drawings in English and Spanish. A proficient bilingual student in an English-dominant preschool setting, Lucretia remained interested and motivated in using her Spanish. If an adult spoke Spanish to her as a way to begin the dictation, Lucretia answered back in Spanish.

7 October: I want to go to the zoo. I like my bike. I want to go
    to the park with my daddy and play in the swings.
5 November: *Yo voy al parque con mi Papi. El me lleva en su
    bicicleta. Yo tengo una hermana y un hermano.*

Plate 1. Leilani's Suns and Designs

Plate 2. Sarina's SpongeBob SquarePants

Plate 3.
Lupe's Dog Picture and Writing

Plate 4.
Paris' Dog Picture and Writing

Plate 5. Isabel's Powerpuff Girls

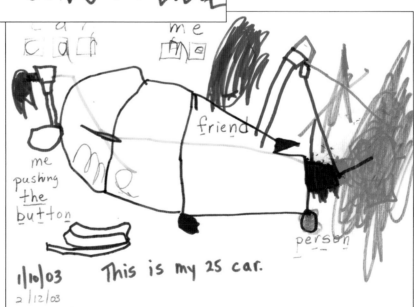

Plate 6.
Emile's 25 Car

April 24: My sister went camping. My mom said I can go
camping too with my friends. I went to the zoo, too. I
have one car. I play with my cars everyday.

Lucretia created a yearlong journal by dictating in Spanish and English, which allowed her to make connections in both languages around a common theme of family experiences, places, and people.

Use Literacy Resources with English-Language Learners

Dictation can place undue pressure on English-language learners, pushing them to know and produce oral language that they are unable or not ready for. One strategy to alleviate this potential problem is to support their dictation through books and other literacy resources. For example, Angel loved Eric Hill's *Spot* books and identified each animal that was hiding behind the flaps, using this as the content for his dictation, which I then wrote down for him. As a Spanish speaker learning English in an English-medium preschool, he looked for recognizable chunks of oral language to remember and reproduce. The animal books, which showed one-word labels of the animal's names along with the corresponding picture, supported Angel's dictation in English.

September 23: Lions. Elephants. Cheetahs. Bears. Caterpillars.
Sharks. Snakes.
October 7: Sharks! Big, small, in the water.
October 13: *Tiburones*. Puppies. Monkeys. Lions. Bears.
Snakes. Hippos. Alligator. Penguins. Turtle.
March 17: Hens. Chickens. Fish. Dinosaurs. Cheetahs. Turtles.
Ladybugs. Monkeys. Pigs.

His strategy of using the animals from the books as one-word responses matched his English-language development at that time. In effect, he devised a self-scaffolding strategy for his dictation.

Encourage Self and Peer-to-Peer Dictation

Children, even in preschool, like to do their own dictation—either on their own or with peers. In this version, one child will tell another child what he or she wants to say for his or her dictation, and the child writes it down either in conventional spelling or in random, "pretend" letters and words. (On occasion, children write down their own dictation by themselves.) In this process, the dictation activity becomes an important factor in social cohesion and forging children's literacy collaboration. This child-controlled strategy has several advantages for promoting early literacy knowledge:

- When children write down their own dictation, they essentially bypass adult assistance and provide their own self-scaffolding and peer-to-peer scaffolding.
- They provide themselves with instant evidence of their ability to record their own dictation.
- They love using my "special dictation pen" to write down their dictation.
- They respond in developmentally and culturally responsive ways with one another, often in ways that I as their teacher would not think of using.
- While some children are recording their own dictation, I am free to do something else with the other children.
- It still allows children the opportunity to "read back" their dictation with me, and if I see fit, I can add my writing in "correct" English.
- It encourages children to interact with one another, talking about what to dictate, how to write it, and how their dictation connects to their drawings.
- Self-dictation encourages language-rich interactions between English-language learners and speakers of varied Englishes.
- It promotes first-language conversation for English-language learners and bilingual speakers.

Artisha, a preschooler, wrote several lines of random letters to make "real" words and sentences and then several lines of squiggly shapes that resembled adult writing. In doing so, she accomplished two things at once: her own writing (the pseudowords and sentences in her own letter writing) and her own dictation (the squiggly lines that resembled adult writing). At the end of her writing, she informed me, "I did my dictation by myself." I wrote down this sentence as yet another layer of dictation (which would help remind me of the significance of her squiggle writing).

On another occasion, Ariel, an African American preschooler, remarked, "I know how to do my own dictation." I replied, "Can you do the dictation for Latisha?" Both Ariel and Latisha readily agreed to this arrangement. So with Ariel standing by, Latisha dictated a short text, which Ariel wrote down as

IRGTH
APTRS
s ^ 4 8

Ariel then got the idea to find Latisha's name card, bring it over to Latisha's journal, and write "By Latisha" at the bottom of Latisha's dictated text (and Ariel's writing).

After this occasion, Ariel became the dictation person whom other children went to. Ariel loved it. Another time, Ariel took down dictation for Susana and Cristina, both English-language learners.

ARIEL: I'm not playing with you! (Susana was a bit slow in getting her journal page open for Ariel)

SUSANA: Barbies. (Ariel wrote down C-A-T to represent Susana's one-word dictation of "Barbies")

ARIEL: Now you got CAT. What else do you want? One more thing.

SUSANA: Books. (Ariel wrote down a string of letters in Ariel's journal)

ARIEL: Do you also want a Christmas star? (Susana nodded yes and Ariel wrote some more, before moving over to help Cristina)

CRISTINA: Jojo.

ARIEL: You want Teja?

CRISTINA: No.

ARIEL: (To me) Cristina said, "Write Jojo bigger! Big girl!" (She wrote a string of letters down on Cristina's page)

MR. MEIER: Who's Jojo?

CRISTINA: My kitty cat.

ARIEL: Come on, Cristina!

CRISTINA: Baby. (She pointed to Ariel's writing)

ARIEL: No, that's big girl.

CRISTINA: A, b, c . . . (She started to sing ABC song)

ARIEL: Hey, I can't hear. (Now to me . . .) She wants me to write "I love you" over here. (Ariel wrote more) Cristina got everything she needed (said to me). She's done. Now I'm ready for my own dictation.

When children themselves take the initiative and control taking down one another's dictation, it's a developmentally appropriate version of the adult process and one that also promotes social collaboration around language and literacy.

Writing and reading are complementary processes and, as such, need to be connected and integrated in classroom life. Children need to see themselves as strong and powerful writers and readers, interested in engaging with texts they write and dictate and those that they read and interpret. Promoting memories for writing for young children is based upon how well writing activities are embedded within the social and intellectual fabric of the classroom. Most often, children write and dictate and talk in literacy activities because these actions bring them closer to their classmates and to us. Fostering memories for writing, then, involves linking attention to written language forms and knowledge with children's powerful interest in learning about themselves and one another. For English-language learn-

ers, producing words and phrases and text in a new language is a challenge—
these children need a supportive environment and specific strategies that
connect writing, drawing, visuals, books, and other literacy resources with
social collaboration and scaffolding from peers and adults. Just as Huma
excitedly and carefully copied down each child's name in her kindergarten
class, English-language learners grow and learn word by word, name by
name, in close connection with literacy and others.

SUGGESTED ACTIVITIES

1. If you work with children who speak African American English, collect their
   journal writings and other examples of writing. Record (either by audiotape
   or writing by hand in your teaching journal) the oral language conversations that accompany their writings. Make a comparative chart of elements
   of African American English and forms of Standard English in the children's
   oral and written language. What language forms stand out? What are the
   functions of these forms for informing, telling, expressing, hypothesizing,
   questioning? Consider ways to point out to children how they can crossover and extend their knowledge of their varied forms of English.
2. Make a web of all the various kinds of writing that you do–or would like to
   do–in your classroom. Then give each activity a code (S = self-scaffolding,
   PP = peer-to-peer scaffolding, TC = teacher-to-child scaffolding, O = other
   scaffolding). Look for an even distribution of these kinds of scaffolding strategies in your writing activities. If there is not a somewhat even spread,
   consider ways to increase varied scaffolding support for your children's
   writing.
3. If you work with English-language learners, what kinds of support are they
   receiving through linking art, writing, dictation, talk, and social interaction? Does this happen on a daily basis, and do the children understand
   the routine and procedures for making these connections? Collect the journals and other forms of writings of a few English-language learners. Make
   a chart showing categories–Writing, Drawing, Dictation, Conversation, and
   Interaction–on a large piece of paper. Make notes as evidence under each
   column–for example, under Conversation, "loves to talk with Manuel about
   his spaceships"; under Writing, "strings of pseudowords in English"; under
   Interaction, "helps Yonatan spell family words." If there are gaps in evidence for any columns, consider new and effective ways to make more
   connections and linkages for your children across and between the
   columns.
4. If you are doing dictation in your classroom, make a web of all your dictation strategies and activities. Are there varied strategies that support all
   the children in your room? If not, choose some new strategies from this
   chapter, consider how they might be implemented, and then try out one
   or two to start. Observe and document your success in achieving your

hoped-for changes in the children's linking of oral and written language through dictation.

USEFUL RESOURCES

Early Writing Development

Bissex, G. (1980). *GNYS AT WRK: A child learns to read and write.* Cambridge, MA: Harvard University Press.

Britton, J. (1983). Writing and the story world. In B. M. Kroll & G. Wells (Eds.), *Explorations in the development of writing* (pp. 3–30). London: John Wiley & Sons.

Chomsky, C. (1971). Write first, read later. *Childhood Education, 47,* 296–299.

Clay, M. (1975). *What did I write?* Portsmouth, NH: Heinemann.

Clay, M. (1987). *Writing begins at home.* Portsmouth, NH: Heinemann.

Dyson, A. H. (1993). *Social worlds of children learning to write in an urban primary school.* New York: Teachers College Press.

Dyson, A. H. (2003). *The brothers and sisters learn to write: Popular literacies in childhood and school cultures.* New York: Teachers College Press.

Graves, D. (1981). *Writers at work.* Portsmouth, NH: Heinemann.

Greenberg, P. (1998). Some thoughts about phonics, feelings, Don Quixote, diversity, and democracy: Teaching young children to read, write, and spell (Part 1). *Young Children, 53*(4), 72–82.

Dictation

Cazden, C. B. & Michaels, S. (1986). Teacher/child collaboration as oral preparation for literacy. In B. B. Schieffelin & P. Gilmore (Eds.), *The acquisition of literacy: Ethnographic perspectives* (pp. 132–153). Norwood, NJ: Ablex.

Cook-Gumperz, J., & Gumperz, J. J. (1981). From oral to written culture: The transition to literacy. In M. F. Whiteman (Ed.), *Variation in writing: Functional and linguistic-cultural differences* (pp. 89–109). Hillsdale, NJ: Erlbaum.

Donaldson, M. (1984). Speech and writing and modes of learning. In H. Goelman, A. Oberg, & F. Smith (Eds.), *Awakening to literacy* (pp. 174–185). Exeter, NH: Heinemann.

Dyson, A. H. (1988). Appreciate the drawing and dictating of young children. *Young Children, 43*(3), 25–32.

Hildyard, A., & Hidi, S. (1985). Oral-written differences in the production and recall of narratives. In D. R. Olson, N. Torrance, & A. Hildyard (Eds.), *Literacy, language, and learning* (pp. 285–307). New York: Cambridge University Press.

Holdaway, D. (1979). *Foundations of literacy.* New York: Ashton Scholastic.

King, M. L., & Rentel, V. M. (1981a). Conveying meaning in written texts. *Language Arts, 58*(6), 721–728.

King, M. L., & Rentel, V. M. (1981b). *How children learn to write: A longitudinal study.* Columbus: Ohio State University Press.

McNamee, G. D. (1990). The social origins of narrative. In M. Hickman (Ed.), *Social and functional approaches to language and thought* (pp. 287–304). New York: Academic Press.

Sulzby, E. (1987). Children's development of prosodic distinctions in telling and dictation modes. In A. Matsuhashi (Ed.), *Writing in real time: Modeling production processes* (pp. 133–160). Norwood, NJ: Ablex.

Children's Book Cited in Chapter 5

Hill, E. (1991). *Spot goes to the park*. New York: G.P. Putnam's Sons.

Chapter 6

Toward New Memories:
Crossing Borders

MR. MEIER: You (Jasmine) can help Alexis read it.
JASMINE: I can't read!
MR. MEIER: Look at the pictures and tell the story.
JASMINE: (hands in the air) Oh, I can't!
MR. MEIER: Just give it a try.
JASMINE: Oh, Ok.

In this book I consolidate and explain philosophies, programs, ideas, and strategies for promoting young children's first- and second-language and literacy learning. We know enough now about literacy education to maintain a concerted effort to connect and strengthen children's literacy learning in preschool and kindergarten. If all our educational research and in-service workshops suddenly ground to a halt, and we started to sift through what we already know and what is already out there, we would find enough good ideas, strategies, materials, and books to strengthen our literacy teaching over time.

We don't need to think outside the box. We need to think *inside* the box, inside the classroom we already have. We need to collaborate, share our knowledge of how and why children become readers and writers, and carefully and sensitively adapt this learning to our own particular teaching and learning settings. This is a tall order. It means that we must begin crossing borders—between preschool and kindergarten, play-based and academic-based programs, oral language learning and written-language learning, monolingual and multilingual modalities, Standard English and varieties of Englishes, monocultural and multicultural contexts, developmentally appropriate and culturally responsive approaches, teaching and assessment, novice and veteran teacher, and teachers and families. This makes for a more realistic and complicated view of improving our literacy education—not an elusive search for the one single best method for literacy teaching. Either fortunately or unfortunately, such a method does not exist. Rather, by crossing the kinds of borders I have described, we can create and fashion our own ideas and strategies and programs that fit our needs and those of our children and families.

BUILDING ON OUR MEMORIES

In this type of border crossing, we can first revisit our own memories for language and literacy learning. We can see and hear again the sights, sounds, words, stories, and books of our childhoods and adulthoods—whether these be positive, painful, exciting, confusing, motivating, or comforting. And we can do this on a continual basis, for how we define literacy and literacy education is forever changing in light of who we are and who we want to become in relation to others. One of my graduate students, a teacher-to-be, did a project on her memories of literacy from childhood. She talked about her memories of moving from the Philippines to the United States as a child, and of her first love for a book in English by her favorite author, Shel Silverstein. She loved Silverstein's rhymes and drawings. But her grandfather disapproved, believing that Silverstein's poetry was not suitable reading material. My student was upset and disappointed. Over time, though, she convinced her grandfather of the value of her favorite author, and her grandfather ultimately agreed with her. Remembering and replaying this memory helped this student and the other students in the class affirm the power of literacy memories as a transformative influence on our teaching and learning.

The current emphasis on literacy goals and standards in preschool and kindergarten would have us believe that literacy teaching is a mechanical process of teaching discrete skills. But it is not. Rather, literacy education is an art. And as an artistic endeavor, our personal experiences and memories for literacy from school, home, and community influence our literacy teaching. This is where we start. Through the prism of our memories for literacy, we can adjust our teaching visions, goals, resources, and strategies to support our students and their families. We need to link literacy education with how we began as readers, writers, talkers, thinkers, and artists.

Currently, we have literacy goals, expectations, and teaching techniques peculiar to preschool, kindergarten, and the primary grades. While this helps focus on literacy goals and strategies for specific developmental stages of learning, there is too much diversity of literacy experiences and knowledge even with a group of 10 5-year-olds. Instead, we need to cross professional borders and reconceptualize early literacy learning to span preschool, kindergarten, and first grade. In this model, preschool and primary-grade teachers envision and implement literacy education for 3- to 8-year-olds and lengthen the developmental and *learning time* that we expect children to experience in their language and literacy. This in turn lengthens the *teaching time* in which we are "expected" to instruct children and help them become powerful readers and writers. As it stands now, there is too much pressure on young children to learn within a short, specified time, and too much pressure on us to teach children to read and write over the span of a year or 182 days.

LITERACY THAT SPEAKS TO CHILDREN

I was watching a children's television show with my preschool-aged daughter. On the screen was a series of rhyming words—*jam Sam ram clam Pam swam scram*—with the first letter or letters highlighted in white and the *am* part in green. There were a few animal characters that interacted during this rhyming activity. I asked my daughter who the elephant character was, and she replied, "Swam," the word she heard and saw on the screen. The following segment had an animal character playing the number chosen for the day, 16, on the organ. When he reached 16, the number 16 arrived on the screen like a pageant winner, followed by such images as 16 pigs doing gymnastics. I thought about my daughter's response of "swam" and the 16 dancing pigs, and realized how hard it is to connect language, literacy, and numeracy for children. It is difficult to know how and why children come to literacy and how they make sense of it (hence the linking of "swam" with the characters) along a developmental continuum.

This television show, like many literacy and numeracy programs and projects, is designed to impart literacy knowledge and motivate curiosity and engagement across children's disparate experiences with literacy. They are designed to help large groups of young children to become readers and writers. And this is fine. Yet in our rush to do this, we lose sight of the ultimate prize of particularizing literacy to children's particular lives, hopes, dreams, feelings, ideas, and expectations. Children need us to present literacy as it fits and broadens their ever-expanding worlds of childhood. A 4-year-old watching a children's television program benefits from some attention to basic literacy knowledge, but will ultimately benefit more fully through literacy experiences that speak to their lives. This is what builds memories for words and literacy—when children find literacy as a welcome stepping stone toward friendships, insights and ideas, funny jokes, cool drawings, crazy characters, silly poems, scary stories.

And this touches our teaching. For children to grab hold of literacy—of books and words and sentences and characters and plots—it needs to grab them and pull them along for their entire lives. We need to foster a lifelong appreciation for and skill in reading and writing, and for interpreting and using our own texts and those of others. Literacy teaching that is momentary is fine—we can focus on figuring out the letter for the short *a* sound in *cat*, but this must be connected with some larger and more sophisticated path for children. Literacy must be something that children can carry along with them as they learn about elephants, the ocean, the sky, friendship, architecture, Day of the Dead/Día de los Muertos, languages, shadows, folktales, poems, artists, authors. Children need large chunks of language and literacy and they need it in large chunks of our varied Englishes, Spanish, Chinese, Vietnamese, and other languages.

Only when we provide rich and interesting possibilities and opportunities for moving along this kind of path do children feel that literacy will take them where they want to go. While rhyming *Sam* and *ram* can delight the ear and children's newly developing sense of linking words, the memory for this delight in language will only take root and flourish within something larger and more important—a book, a story, friends, adults, conversation, thoughts and feelings, questions, stories. It is only in this richly textured swirl of the stuff of childhood that we can find and promote lifelong memories for words and literacy.

Appendix A

Language and Literacy Development Profile (LLDP)—3-Year-Olds

Child's Name: _____   D.O.B.: _____

Languages Spoken at Home: _____

Your child shows evidence of the language and literacy learning checked below.

Language Development	Literacy Development
FALL	
____ speaks clearly ____ describes objects ____ engages in dramatic play ____ follows 1-step directions ____ uses words to communicate with peers ____ initiates play using words ____ communicates with adults ____ listens to oral stories ____ listens to songs/fingerplays	____ notices books ____ looks at books with adults/peers ____ holds book right side up ____ listens to stories and books ____ listens to audiotaped stories ____ turns pages from left to right ____ grasps paint brush ____ grasps markers or crayons
SPRING	
____ describes actions ____ recites words to fingerplays/songs ____ uses language to play cooperatively ____ solves conflicts through talking ____ recognizes basic colors ____ participates in group discussions ____ understands stories at story time ____ sequences 2 events ____ participates in songs/fingerplays ____ participates in rhyming games ____ learns new words (bilingual language development)	____ tells story from pictures in book ____ selects books independently ____ uses puppets/props with books ____ manipulates uppercase letters ____ scribbles when drawing ____ dictates labels/words for drawings ____ makes meaningful marks on a page

Additional Teacher Comments (child's interests, creativity, curiosity):

Teacher's Signature: _____   Date: _____

Parent/Guardian's Signature: _____

Appendix A *(cont'd)*

Language and Literacy Development Profile (LLDP)—4- and 5-Year-Olds

Child's Name: _____   D.O.B.: _____

Languages Spoken at Home: _____

Your child shows evidence of the language and literacy learning checked below.

Language Development	*Literacy Development*
FALL	
___ describes experiences	___ turns pages one at a time
___ follows 2-step directions	___ dictates a label for a picture
___ initiates songs and fingerplays	___ chooses one or more books independently
___ participates in group story time	___ "reads" from top to bottom
___ rhymes simple words	___ selects story and informational books
___ sequences simple events	___ retells stories
___ tells own stories	___ manipulates lowercase letters
___ asks questions	___ shows interest in writing first name
___ participates in story dramatization	___ makes random marks for writing
SPRING	
___ uses language to solve conflicts	___ identifies 5 letters of the alphabet
___ sequences 2–3 events	___ recognizes letters in own name
___ uses more complex sentences	___ talks about letter sounds
___ makes predictions	___ recognizes numerals 1, 2, 3, 4, 5
___ guesses and estimates	___ draws picture of self
___ uses new words in context (bilingual)	___ uses computer
___ understands phrases (bilingual)	___ "reads" bilingual books
___ understands sentences (bilingual)	___ "reads" back random written marks

Additional Teacher Comments (child's interests, creativity, curiosity, learning):

Teacher's Signature: _____   Date: _____

Parent/Guardian's Signature: _____

Appendix B

Preschool to Kindergarten Communication Sheet (PKCS)

Date: _____ Preschool Teacher's Name: _____

Site/Room #: _____ Tel.: _____ E-mail: _____

Language(s) of Instruction: English and/or _____

Child's Name: _____ D.O.B: _____

Current Age: _____ Language(s) Spoken at Home: _____

1. Did the child receive special instructional and support services (such as speech and language support)?

   yes _____(IEP attached)   no _____

   Services received: _____

2. Any special health concerns (mobility, sight, hearing, etc.)?

   yes _____   no _____

   If yes, list as _____

3. Any special dietary/nutrition concerns?

   yes _____   no _____

   If yes, list as _____

4. Overall Language and Literacy Development (see attached LLDP form):

5. Second Language and Bilingual Proficiency (see attached LLDP form):

Appendix B *(cont'd)*

6. Fine- and Gross-Motor Skills:

7. Social Interaction and Focusing (circle relevant items and explain with examples):

    Listens/participates at whole-group time

    Plays with others

    Plays independently

    Follows directions

    Understands classroom routines

    Cleans up and follows transitions

8. Favorite Classroom Activities (Indoor and Outdoor):

9. Attendance and Relevant Family Information:

10. Other:

References

Ada, A. F. (1988). The pajaro valley experience: Working with Spanish-speaking parents to develop children's reading and writing skills in the home through the use of children's literature. In T. Skutnabb-Kangas & J. Cummins (Eds.), *Minority education—From shame to struggle* (pp. 223–238). Philadelphia, PA: Multi-Lingual Matters.

Ada, A. F. (1989). *Language arts through children's literature: Using children's books to develop critical thinking and expression.* Emeryville, CA: Children's Book Press.

Ada, A. F. (2003). *A magical encounter: Latino children's literature in the classroom.* Boston, MA: Allyn and Bacon.

Adams, M. J. (1990). *Beginning to read: Thinking and learning about print.* Cambridge, MA: MIT Press.

Applebee, A. N. (1978). *The child's concept of story: Ages two to seventeen.* Chicago, IL: University of Chicago Press.

Baker, C. (2000). *A parents' and teachers' guide to bilingualism* (2nd ed.). London: Multilingual Matters.

Ballenger, C. (1999). *Teaching other people's children: Literacy and learning in a bilingual classroom.* New York: Teachers College Press.

Baugh, J. (1999). *Out of the mouths of slaves: African American language and educational malpractice.* Austin, TX: University of Texas Press.

Beck, I. L., McKeown, M. G., & Kucan, L. (2003). Taking delight in words: Using oral language to build young children's vocabularies. *American Educator, 27*(1), 36–41, 45–48.

Berk, L. E. (1994, November). Why children talk to themselves. *Scientific American,* pp. 78–83.

Bishop, R. S. (1990). Walk tall in the world: African American literature for today's children. *Journal of Negro Education, 59*(4), 556–565.

Bissex, G. (1980). *GNYS AT WRK: A child learns to read and write.* Cambridge, MA: Harvard University Press.

Bowman, B. (Ed.). (2003). *Love to read: Essays on developing and enhancing early literacy skills of African American children.* Washington, DC: National Association for the Education of Young Children.

Bredekamp, S., & Copple, C. (Eds.). (1997). *Developmentally appropriate practice in early childhood programs* (rev. ed.). Washington, DC: National Association for the Education of Young Children.

Bredekamp, S., Copple, C., & Neuman, S. B. (2000). *Learning to read and write: Developmentally appropriate practices for young children.* Washington, DC: National Association for the Education of Young Children.

Bredekamp, S. & Neuman, S. B. (2000). Becoming a reader: A developmentally appropriate approach. In D. S. Strickland & L. M. Morrow (Eds.), *Beginning reading and writing* (pp. 22–35). New York: Teachers College Press.

Britton, J. (1983). Writing and the story world. In B. M. Kroll & G. Wells (Eds.), *Explorations in the development of writing* (pp. 3–30). London: John Wiley & Sons.

Burnaford, G., Fischer, J., & Hobson, D. (Eds.). (2001). *Teachers doing research: The power of action through inquiry*. Manwah, NJ: Lawrence Erlbaum Associates.

Bussis, A., Chittenden, E., Amarel, M., & Klausner, E. (1985). *Inquiry into meaning.* Hillsdale, NJ: Earlbaum.

Cadwell, L. B. (2003). *Bringing learning to life: The Reggio approach to early childhood education*. New York: Teachers College Press.

Cai, M., & Bishop, R. S. (1994). Multicultural literature for children: Towards a clarification of the concept. In A. H. Dyson & C. Genishi (Eds.), *The need for story: Cultural diversity in classroom and community* (pp. 57–71). Urbana, IL: National Council of Teachers of English.

California Child Development Division for Desired Results for Preschool. http://www.cde.ca.gov/cyfsbranch/child_development/

California Department of Education for Kindergarten. http://www.cde.ca.gov/standards/

California Department of Education. (1998). *Assessing the development of a first and a second language in early childhood*. Sacramento: California Department of Education.

Carter, M., & Curtis, D. (2003). *Designs for living and learning: Transforming early childhood environments*. St. Paul, MN: Redleaf.

Cazden, C. B., & Michaels, S. (1986). Teacher/child collaboration as oral preparation for literacy. In B. B. Schieffelin & P. Gilmore (Eds.), *The acquisition of literacy: Ethnographic perspectives* (pp. 132–153). Norwood, NJ: Ablex.

Champion, T. B. (2003). *Understanding storytelling among African American children: A journey from Africa to America*. Mahwah, NJ: Lawrence Erlbaum.

Chomsky, C. (1971). Write first, read later. *Childhood Education, 47*, 296–299.

Clay, M. (1975). *What did I write?* Portsmouth, NH: Heinemann.

Clay, M. (1985). *The early detection of reading difficulties* (3rd ed.). Auckland, NZ: Heinemann.

Clay, M. (1987). *Writing begins at home*. Portsmouth, NH: Heinemann.

Clay, M. (1993). *An observation survey of early literacy achievement*. Portsmouth, NH: Heinemann.

Clay, M. (1998). *By different paths to common outcomes*. York, ME: Stenhouse.

Clay, M. (2000). *Concepts about print for teachers of young children*. Auckland, NZ: Heinemann.

Clay, M. (2000). *Running records for classroom teachers*. Auckland, NZ: Heinemann.

Clay, M. (2001). *Change over time in children's literacy development*. Auckland, NZ: Heinemann.

Cochran-Smith, M., & Lytle, S. (1993). *Inside/outside—Teacher research and knowledge.* New York: Teachers College Press.

Cohen, D. H., Stern, V., & Balaban, N. (1997). *Observing and recording the behavior of young children*. New York: Teachers College Press.

Compton-Lilly, C. (2003). *Reading families: The literate lives of urban children*. New York: Teachers College Press.

Cook, J. W. (2001). Create and tell a story: Help young children who have psychological difficulties. *Young Children, 56*(1), 67–70.

Cook-Gumperz, J., & Gumperz, J. J. (1981). From oral to written culture: The transition to literacy. In M. F. Whiteman (Ed.), *Variation in writing: Functional and linguistic-cultural differences* (pp. 89–109). Hillsdale, NJ: Erlbaum.

Cummins, J. (1996). *Negotiating identities: Education for empowerment in a diverse society*. Ontario, CA: California Association for Bilingual Education.

Darder, A., Torres, R. D., & Gutíerrez, H. (Eds). (1997). *Latinos and education: A critical reader*. New York: Routledge.

de Boysson-Bardies, B. (1999). *How language comes to children: From birth to two years*. Cambridge, MA: MIT Press.

Delgado-Gaitan, C. (1990). *Literacy for empowerment: The role of parents in children's education*. New York: Falmer Press.

Delpit, L. (1995). *Other people's children: Cultural conflict in the classroom*. New York: The Free Press.

Dickinson, D. K., & Tabors, P. O. (2002). Fostering language and literacy in classrooms and homes. *Young Children, 57*(2), 10–19.

Diller, D. (2003). *Literacy work stations: Making centers work*. York, ME: Stenhouse.

Ditzel, R. J. (2000). *Great beginnings: Creating a literacy-rich kindergarten*. York, ME: Stenhouse.

Donaldson, M. (1984). Speech and writing and modes of learning. In H. Goelman, A. Oberg, & F. Smith (Eds.). *Awakening to literacy* (pp. 174–185). Exeter, NH: Heinemann.

Dragon, P. B. (2001). *Literacy from day one*. Portsmouth, NH: Heinemann.

Drummond, M. J. (1994). *Learning to see: Assessment through observation*. York, ME: Stenhouse.

Duke, N. K. (2003). Reading to learn from the very beginning: Information books in early childhood. *Young Children, 58*(2), 14–20.

Dyson, A. H. (1988). Appreciate the drawing and dictating of young children. *Young Children, 43*(3), 25–32.

Dyson, A. H. (1993). *Social worlds of children learning to write in an urban primary school*. New York: Teachers College Press.

Dyson, A. H. (2003). *The brothers and sisters learn to write: Popular literacies in childhood and school cultures*. New York: Teachers College Press.

Dyson, A. H., & Genishi, C. (Eds.). (1994). *The need for story: Cultural diversity in classroom and community*. Urbana, IL: National Council of Teachers of English.

Edwards, C., Gandini, L., & Forman, G. (Eds.). (1998). *The hundred languages of children: The Reggio Emilia approach to early childhood education* (2nd ed.). Norwood, NJ: Ablex.

Engel, S. (1995). *The stories children tell: Making sense of the narratives of childhood*. New York: W. H. Freeman.

Espiritu, E., Meier, D. R., Villazana-Price, N., & Wong, M. (2002). Promoting teacher research in early childhood: A collaborative project on children's language and literacy learning. *Young Children, 57*(5), 71–79.

Ferreiro, E., & Teberosky, A. (1982). *Literacy before schooling*. Exeter, NH: Heinemann.

Fillmore, L. W. (1979). Individual differences in second language acquisition. In C. J. Fillmore, D. K. William, & S. Y. Wang, (Eds.). *Individual differences in language ability and language behavior* (pp. 30–49). New York: Academic Press.

Fillmore, L. W. (1991). When learning a second language means losing the first. *Early Childhood Research Quarterly 6*(3), 323–346.

Fountas, I. C., & Pinnell, G. S. (1996). *Guided reading: Good first teaching for all children*. Portsmouth, NH: Heinemann.

Freeman, D. (1998). *Doing teacher research: From inquiry to understanding*. New York: Heinle & Heinle.

Gadsden, V. G. (1994). Understanding family literacy: Conceptual issues facing the field. *Teachers College Record, 96*(1), 78–89.

García, E. (1994). *Understanding and meeting the challenge of student cultural diversity*. Boston, MA: Houghton Mifflin.

Gardner, H., Feldman, D. H., & Krechevsky, M. (1998). *Building on children's strengths: The exploration of project spectrum, Vol. 1*. New York: Teachers College Press. Available: http://ericee.org/project.html

Gardner, H., Feldman, D. H., & Krechevsky, M. (1998). *Project Zero frameworks: Preschool assessment handbook, Vol. 3*. New York: Teachers College Press.

Genesee, F. (Ed.). (1994). *Educating second language children: The whole child, the whole curriculum, the whole community*. New York: Cambridge University Press.

Genishi, C. (2002). Young English language learners: Resourceful in the classroom. *Young Children, 57*(4), 66–71.

Genishi, C., & Brainard, M. (1995). Assessment of bilingual children: A dilemma seeking solutions. In E. García & B. McLaughlin (Eds.), *Meeting the challenge of linguistic and cultural diversity in early childhood education* (pp. 49–63). New York: Teachers College Press.

Genishi, C., & Dyson, A. H. (1984). *Language assessment in the early years*. Cambridge, MA: Harvard University Press.

Genishi, C., Yung-Chan, D., & Stires, S. (2000). Talking their way into print: English language learners in a prekindergarten classroom. In D. S. Strickland, & L. M. Morrow (Eds.), *Beginning reading and writing* (pp. 66–80). New York: Teachers College Press.

Golinkoff, R. M., & Hirsh-Pasek, K. (1999). *How babies talk*. New York: Dutton.

Graves, D. (1981). *Writers at work*. Portsmouth, NH: Heinemann.

Greenberg, P. (1998). Some thoughts about phonics, feelings, Don Quixote, diversity, and democracy: Teaching young children to read, write, and spell (Part 1). *Young Children, 53*(4), 72–82.

Gregory, E. (1996). *Making sense of a new world: Learning to read in a second language*. London: Paul Chapman.

Gregory, E. (2001). Sisters and brothers as language and literacy teachers: Synergy between siblings playing and working together. *Journal of Early Childhood Literacy, 1*(3), 301–322.

Gregory, E., Long, S., & Volk, D. (Eds.). (2004). *Many pathways to literacy: Learning with siblings, grandparents, peers, and communities*. London: Routledge.

Gullo, D. (1993). *Understanding assessment and evaluation in early childhood education*. New York: Teachers College Press.

Hakuta, K. (1986). *Mirror of language: The debate on bilingualism*. New York: Basic Books.

Harp, B., & Brewer, J. A. (2000). Assessing reading and writing in the early years. In D. S. Strickland & L. M. Morrow (Eds.), *Beginning reading and writing* (pp. 154–167). New York: Teachers College Press.

Harris, V. (Ed.). (1993). *Teaching multicultural literature in grades K–8*. Norwood, PA: Christopher Gordon.

Heath, S. B. (1982). What no bedtime story means: Narrative skills at home and school. *Language in Society, 11*(2), 49–76.

Helm, J. H., & Beneke, S. (Eds.). (2003). *The power of projects: Meeting contemporary challenges in early childhood classrooms.* New York: Teachers College Press.

Helm, J. H., Beneke, S., & Steinheimer, K. (1998). *Windows on learning: Documenting young children's work.* New York: Teachers College Press.

Hiebert, E. H., & Taylor, B. M. (Eds.). (1995). *Getting reading right from the start: Effective early literacy interventions.* Boston: Allyn & Bacon.

Hildyard, A., & Hidi, S. (1985). Oral-written differences in the production and recall of narratives. In D. R. Olson, N. Torrance, & A. Hildyard (Eds.), *Literacy, language, and learning* (pp. 285–307). New York: Cambridge University Press.

Himley, M., & Carini, P. F. (Eds.). (2000). *From another angle: Children's strengths and school standards, the Prospect Center's descriptive review of the child.* New York: Teachers College Press.

Holdaway, D. (1979). *Foundations of literacy.* New York: Ashton Scholastic.

Houle, A., & Krogress, A. (2001). The wonders of word walls. *Young Children, 56*(5), 92–95.

Hubbard, R. S., & Power, B. M. (1999). *Living the questions: A guide for teacher-researchers.* York, ME: Stenhouse.

Igoa, C. (1995). *The inner world of the immigrant child.* Mahwah, NJ: Lawrence Erlbaum.

Isbell, R. T. (2002). Telling and retelling stories: Learning language and literacy. *Young Children, 57*(2), 26–30.

Jipson, J. (1991). Developmentally appropriate practice: Culture, curriculum, connections. *Early Education and Development, 2*(2), 120–136.

Johnston, P. H. (2000). *Running records: A self-tutoring guide.* York, ME: Stenhouse.

Katz, L., & Chard, S. (1989). *Engaging children's minds: The project approach.* Greenwich, CT: Ablex.

Kennedy, D. K. (1996). After Reggio Emilia: May the conversation begin. *Young Children, 51*(5), 24–27.

King, M. L., & Rentel, V. M. (1981a). Conveying meaning in written texts. *Language Arts, 58*(6), 721–728.

King, M. L., & Rentel, V. M. (1981b). *How children learn to write: A longitudinal study.* Columbus, OH: Ohio State University.

Koralek, D. (Ed.). (2003). *Spotlight on young children and oral language.* Washington, DC: National Association for the Education of Young Children.

Krashen, S. (1985). *The input hypothesis.* Oxford, UK: Pergamon.

Krashen, S. (1999). *Condemned without a trial: Bogus arguments against bilingualism.* Portsmouth, NH: Heinemann.

Kratcoski, A. M., & Katz, K. B. (1998). Conversing with young language learners in the classroom. *Young Children, 53*(3), 30–33.

Labov, W. (1977). *Language in the inner city: Studies in the Black English vernacular.* Philadelphia: University of Pennsylvania Press.

Ladson-Billings, G. (1994). *The dreamkeepers: Successful teachers of African American children.* San Francisco, CA: Jossey-Bass.

Lee, C. D. (1994). African-centered pedagogy: Complexities and possibilities. In M. J. Shujaa (Ed.), *Too much schooling, too little education: A paradox of Black life in White societies* (pp. 295–318). Trenton, NJ: Africa World Press.

LeeKeenan, D., & Edwards, C. P. (1992). Using the project approach with toddlers. *Young Children, 47*(4), 31–36.

Lindfors, J. (1999). *Children's talk and learning* (2nd ed.). New York: Teachers College Press.

Making learning visible: Children as individual and group learners. (2003). Reggio Emilia, Italy: Reggio Children. (Distributed through the National Association for the Education of Young Children).

Mallory, B. L., & New, R. S. (Eds.). (1994). *Diversity and developmentally appropriate practices: Challenges for early childhood education.* New York: Teachers College Press.

McCaleb, S. P. (1995). *Building communities of learners: A collaboration among teachers, students, families, and community.* Mahwah, NJ: Lawrence Erlbaum.

McNamee, G. D. (1990). The social origins of narrative. In M. Hickman (Ed.), *Social and functional approaches to language and thought* (pp. 287–304). New York: Academic Press.

Meier, D. R. (1997). *Learning in small moments: Life in an urban classroom.* New York: Teachers College Press.

Meier, D. R. (2000). *Scribble scrabble: Learning to read and write with diverse children, teachers, and families.* New York: Teachers College Press.

Miller, P., & Sperry, L. (1988). Early talk about the past: The origins of conversational stories of personal experience. *Journal of Child Language, 15,* 293–315.

Montessori, M. (1964). *The Montessori method.* New York: Shocken Books.

Montessori, M. (1967). *The absorbent mind.* New York: Henry Holt and Company.

Morrow. L. M., & Smith, J. K. (Eds.). (1990). *Assessment for instruction in early literacy.* Englewood Cliffs, NJ: Prentice Hall.

Nelson, K. (1989). *Narratives from the crib.* Cambridge, MA: Harvard University Press.

Neuman, S. B., & Dickinson, D. K. (Eds.). (2001). *The handbook of early literacy research.* New York: The Guilford Press.

Nieto, S. (2002). *Language, culture, and teaching: Critical perspectives for a new century.* Mahwah, NJ: Lawrence Erlbaum.

Ortiz, R., Stile, S., & Brown, C. (1999). Early literacy activities of fathers: Reading and writing with young children. *Young Children, 54*(5), 16–18.

Owocki, G. (1999). *Literacy through play.* Portsmouth, NH: Heinemann.

Paley, V. (1980). *Wally's stories.* Cambridge, MA: Harvard University Press.

Reyes, M. de la Luz, & Halcon, J. (Eds.). (2001). *The best for our children: Critical perspectives on literacy for Latino children.* New York: Teachers College Press.

Rhoten, L., & Lane, M. (2001). More than ABC's: The new alphabet books. *Young Children, 57*(2), 41–45.

Rickford, J. (1999). *African American vernacular English.* Oxford: Basil Blackwell.

Robinson, V., Ross, G., & Neal, H. (2000). *Emergent literacy in kindergarten: A review of the research and related suggested activities and learning strategies.* San Mateo, CA: California Kindergarten Association.

Roskos, K., & Christies, J. (2001). On not pushing too hard: A few contrary remarks about linking literacy and play. *Young Children, 56*(3), 64–66.

Roskos, K. A., Christie, J. F., & Richgels, D. J. (2003). The essentials of early literacy instruction. *Young Children, 58*(2), 52–60.

Sandy, C. S., & Stout, N. S. (2002). Pillow talk: Fostering the emotional language needs of young learners. *Young Children, 57*(2), 20–25.

Schickendanz, J. A. (1993). Designing the early childhood classroom environment to facilitate literacy development. In B. Spodek & O. N. Saracho (Eds.), *Language and literacy in early childhood education: Yearbook in early childhood education* (pp. 141–155). New York: Teachers College Press.

Schon, I. (2000). Delightful books in Spanish for young children. *Young Children, 55*(1), 82–83.

Seefeldt, C. (2002). *Creating rooms of wonder: Valuing and displaying children's work to enhance the learning process.* Beltsville, MD: Gryphon House.

Slapin, B., Seale, D. & Gonzales, R. (2000). *How to tell the difference: A guide to evaluating children's books for anti-Indian bias.* Berkeley, CA: Oyate.

Smitherman, G. (1977). *Talkin and testifyin: The language of Black America.* Boston: Houghton Mifflin.

Snow, C. E., Burns, S., & Griffin, P. (1998). *Preventing reading difficulties in young children.* Washington, DC: National Academy Press.

Spodek, B., & Saracho, O. N. (Eds.), (1993). *Language and literacy in early childhood education: Yearbook in early childhood education, Vol. 4.* New York: Teachers College Press.

Stauffer, R. G. (1970). *The language-experience approach to the teaching of reading.* New York: Harper & Row.

Stauffer, R. G. (1980). *The language-experience approach to the teaching of reading.* (2nd Ed.). New York: Harper & Row.

Stremmel, A. (2002). Nurturing professional and personal growth through inquiry. *Young Children, 57*(5), 62–70.

Stremmel, A. J., Fu, V. R., & Hill, L. T. (Eds.). (2002). *Teaching and learning: Collaborative exploration of the Reggio Emilia approach.* Upper Saddle River, NJ: Merrill/Prentice Hall.

Sulzby, E. (1987). Children's development of prosodic distinctions in telling and dictation modes. In A. Matsuhashi (Ed.), *Writing in real time: Modeling production processes* (pp. 133–160). Norwood, NJ: Ablex.

Tabors, O. (1998). What early childhood educators need to know: Developing effective programs for linguistically and culturally diverse kids and families. *Young Children, 53*(6), 31–42.

Tabors, P. (1997). *One child, two languages: A guide for preschool educators of children learning English as a second language.* Baltimore, MD: Paul H. Brooks.

Taylor, D., & Dorsey-Gaines, C. (1988). *Growing up literate: Learning from inner-city families.* Portsmouth, NH: Heinemann.

Teale, W., & Sulzby, E. (Eds.) (1986). *Emergent literacy: Writing and reading.* Norwood, NJ: Ablex Publishing.

Trelease, J. (1994). *The read-aloud handbook,* (4th Ed.). New York: Penguin.

Valdés, G. (1996). *Con respeto: Bridging the distances between culturally diverse families and schools.* New York: Teachers College Press.

Valdés, G. (2001). *Learning and not learning English: Latino students in American schools.* New York: Teachers College Press.

Vasquez, V. M. (2003). *Negotiating critical literacies with young children.* Mahwah, NJ: Lawrence Erlbaum.

Vygotsky, L. S. (1978). *Mind in society.* Cambridge, MA: Harvard University Press.

Vygotsky, L. S. (1986). *Thought and language.* Cambridge, MA: MIT Press.

Wang, J., Inhoff, A., & Chen, H-C. (1999). *Reading in Chinese script: A cognitive analysis*. Mahwah, NJ: Erlbaum.

Whaley, C. (2002). Meeting the diverse needs of children through storytelling. *Young Children, 57*(2), 31–35.

Xu Hong, S., & Rutledge, A. L. (2003). Kindergartners learn through environmental print. *Young Children, 58*(2), 44–51.

Yopp, H. K. (1995). A test for assessing phonemic awareness in young children. *The Reading Teacher, 1*(49), 20–29.

Index

About the Author

Daniel Meier is associate professor of elementary education at San Francisco State University. He teaches courses in children's language and literacy learning, teacher research, and early childhood education. He holds degrees from Wesleyan University, Harvard University, and the University of California at Berkeley. Meier is the author of *Learning in Small Moments: Life in an Urban Classroom* (Teachers College Press, 1997) and *Scribble Scrabble: Learning to Read and Write with Diverse Teachers, Children, and Families* (Teachers College Press, 2000). Meier has taught preschool, kindergarten, and first grade in both private and public elementary schools. He is currently a part-time kindergarten literacy specialist at an elementary school in the San Francisco Bay Area. The author invites correspondence to Daniel Meier, Department of Elementary Education, San Francisco State University, 1600 Holloway Avenue, San Francisco, CA 94132. E-mail: dmeier@sfsu.edu